25 ICONS OF PEACE
IN THE
QUR'AN

25 ICONS OF PEACE IN THE QUR'AN

Lessons of Harmony

MARY SAAD ASSEL

iUniverse, Inc.
New York Bloomington

iUniverse books may be ordered through booksellers or by contacting:

iUniverse
1663 Liberty Drive
Bloomington, IN 47403
www.iuniverse.com
1-800-Authors (1-800-288-4677)

ISBN: 978-1-4401-6901-4 (sc)
ISBN: 978-1-4401-6902-1 (ebook)
ISBN: 978-1-4401-6903-8 (hc)

Printed in the United States of America

iUniverse rev. date: 03/06/2010

In memory of my son,
Mazen Saleh

Contents

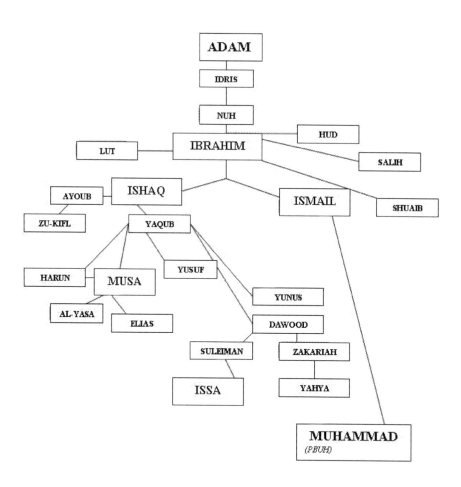

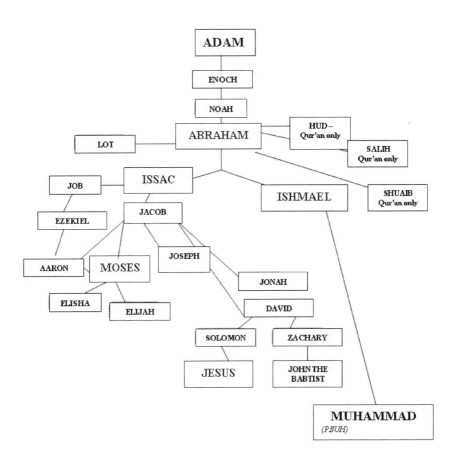

Acknowledgments

When my son Mazen joined the Dominion of God at the age of thirty-three, I searched for universal justification. I craved to find peace and to connect with God, Who would ultimately lead me to him. The burden of sacrificing away the love I had for him to the unknown was difficult and agonizing, and after hours, days, and months of living through the piercing pain of losing him, I reached into the depth of my soul and found solace when I began to connect spiritually and emotionally with God. My readings of the Qur'an and lengthy discussions with numerous religious scholars have helped me find that studying and examining the Qur'an was my road to peace. I felt serenity by reading God's words and realizing that one day I would be reunited with my son.

> "Gardens of perpetual bliss: they shall enter there, as well as the righteous among their fathers, their spouses, and their offspring: and angels shall enter unto them from every gate (with the salutation): "Peace unto you for that ye persevered in patience! Now how excellent is the final home!"[1]

It was Mazen's death that inspired me to gather the stories of the prophets from the Qur'an who repeatedly informed mankind that God will bring us all together on the day of judgment to extend His mercy on us so that we may experience eternal bliss. The stories of the prophets are fascinating and filled with overt and hidden codes that teach us the genuine meaning behind pain, tolerance, love, and peace. It is my aspiration that readers will share my joy in learning more about God's messengers and find the inner harmony that I was able to find through the power of faith and belief in the afterlife.

This is only a small beginning to my spiritual growth and devotion to God. I would like to thank my mother and father whose knowledge, daily recitations, and interpretations of the Qur'an increased my understanding and laid the foundation for me to write this book. I would like to extend a grand series of appreciation to my husband who is my inspiration, editor, and mentor; my siblings, who cheered me through; my daughters Rania, Dania, and their husbands, who supported my idea early on and gave me additional insight; my eleven year-old son Adam who silently grasped the concept that I needed time to myself to complete this book; my daughter-in-law Mona for her support; and certainly my grandchildren for their ongoing inspiration and discussions as they listened to the drafted stories of the prophets during sleepovers.

I extend a great amount of gratitude to Imam and publisher Hassan Qazwini whose guidance and educational and religious expertise gave legitimacy to his editorial comments on Islamic history, the lives of the prophets, and the life of the Prophet Muhammad *(pbuh)*; Hussein Hakim, editor and publisher of numerous books and articles on Islamic jurisprudence for his keen insight and comments; Imam Muhammad Mardini for assisting me in outlining the chronological order of the prophets' lives; Ed Demerly my friend and colleague for his careful edits of my final chapter; and my co-op students Doua Djekidel and Mobeen Muzzammil, as well as my husband and son Adam for validating my quotations and references. Lastly, I am mostly grateful to the years that God granted me my son, Mazen, who will always live with me in spirit, and it is to his memory that I dedicate this book. Even though I am extremely grateful to those who have offered constructive comments and editorial changes, I alone bear responsibility for the contents of this book.

Introduction

Behold! God took the covenant of the prophets, saying: "I give you a Book and Wisdom; then comes to you an apostle, confirming what is with you; do ye believe in him and render him help." God said: "Do ye agree, and take this my Covenant as binding on you?" They said: "We agree." He said: "Then bear witness, and I am with you among the witnesses."[1]

Prior to introducing the Prophets of Islam, it is necessary to define the word *Islam*. *Islam* means "submission." It calls upon people to submit their will to God and to believe in Him as the One and only God. Islam is a monotheistic religion that calls for total submission to the Eternal and Everlasting God. To convey His sovereignty to mankind, God introduced the institution of prophethood, since man can only gain knowledge of God through Divine revelation. The prophets mentioned in the chapters to follow were chosen by God to be His spokesmen and historical representatives. Even though they were most often rejected by their people, the authority of their messages lives to defeat the rejecters and give Islam the ascendancy it carries in the world today.

The importance of religion consists of its capacity to offer the individual or group general conceptions of the world, the self, and the bond between them. It provides a framework of ideas that compels the mind to invite theological reflection and discard rationalism when trying to make sense of the universe and the mystery behind its creation. This book reveals the stories of the prophets and statements of fact from a Muslim's point of view. This is by no means a declaration of the supremacy of one religion over the other, but rather an opportunity to perceive Islam as a peaceful religion and more unified with previous revelations of the stories of the prophets than some perceive it to be. The Qur'an states that even though there are differences among *Ahl Al-kitab* or People of the Book, namely, Christians and Jews, God alone will judge those differences.

> And dispute ye not with the People of the Book, except with means better (than mere disputation), unless it be with those of them who inflict wrong (and injury): but say, "We believe in the revelation which has come down to us and in that which came down to you; Our Allah and your Allah is one; and it is to Him we bow (in Islam)."[2]

According to Muslims, the Qur'an is man's final monotheistic religious text. It is God's word revealed verbatim and seriatim by the Archangel Jibril (Gabriel) to the Prophet Muhammad *(pbuh)*, the last of all prophets. Referred to as "the Sacred Word of God," it is the faithful copy of a text contained in the preexistent heavenly tablet (*Lawh Mahfouz*), God's heavenly Scripture (*Al-kitab*), as referenced throughout the Qur'an. It is God's final message to the world, as it follows and confirms the content of earlier revelations. According to the Qur'an, these earlier revelations were incomplete and misinterpreted. The Qur'an was revealed to Prophet Muhammad *(pbuh)* to correct these misinterpretations and is hence both God's original and eternal Scripture and His last, perfect, and unchangeable revelation to humankind. It teaches believers to trust in God and to follow His doctrine.[3] It teaches that God's messengers are human and that, in order to preach of His existence, they were to endure excruciating sacrifices in one form or another and set forth the example that, to believe in God and the Hereafter and to obtain eternal bliss on the Day of Judgment, they were to sacrifice their freedom and possessions in the name of God and eternal peace. When God created man, His main goal was to create peace and harmony, but when man interrupted such harmony by failing to remember God's request not to approach the specified "tree," the re-institutionalization of peace on earth and belief in the One and Only God became the goal of all prophets in the Qur'an.

God's doctrine, the Qur'an, is simple to read, yet complex. It is difficult to comprehend the exact meaning of certain verses with respect to the certainty of God's intended message in any given chapter *(sura)* or verse *(Ayah)* despite the fact that some might be quite simple and straightforward. It is important to note that repeated readings of the same verse may convey a new and deeper observation of the verse compared to its overall meaning in context. Every letter or expression is broken into segments, and analyzed and interpreted differently by the undertakers of Islamic exegesis. Muslim scholars have differed in opinion, and their differences have led to an evolution of various schools of thought and divisions in the religion. Despite all such critical interpretations, God appeals to every believer, man and woman, young or old, to read the Qur'an repeatedly and to follow its directives religiously, faithfully, and under the example *(sunnah al rasoul)* of Prophet Muhammad *(pbuh)* himself. Even though the Qur'an does not state the exact number of God's messengers, Prophet Muhammad *(pbuh)* was one of the many messengers responsible for spreading God's message and the last to represent the pre-figurations of all others.[4]

To facilitate the reader's prospective research, references and interpretations were taken from both *Shiaa* and *Sunni* schools of thought. This was done to broaden my perspective and to reduce any bias toward one sect or the other. As such, readers of all faiths and sects are invited to examine more closely the complexity of verses as they relate to the stories of the prophets in the Qur'an and those in other sacred texts. Also, after researching and closely examining the interpretations of numerous authors and despite the author's use of archaic English, I have chosen to quote Abdullah Yusuf Ali's *The Holy Qur'an: Text, Translation, and Commentary* because I found his translation to be more in line with the overall Arabic meaning of each verse or chapter. Yusuf Ali's interpretation of the Qur'an was the product of decades of work. It was not a simple, word for word interpretation but rather a solid, unbiased, and objective analysis of the Qur'an in its entirety. He reflected on the tone, rhythm, and harmony of the Arabic word, the ideas of other commentators, and arrived at what appears in my humble opinion to be the most reasonable and acceptable translation. Even though Yusuf occasionally alternated between the use of English and Arabic names of the prophets in his translation of the Qur'an, I will refer to all prophets using their Arabic surnames. In addition and for clarification purposes, I have added the name of the speaker prior to each quote. Note that God is addressing Prophet Muhammad *(pbuh)* wherever the speaker is introduced with "Say."

The stories, as they currently exist in the Qur'an, are not written with a beginning, middle, and end. In fact, the story of Prophet Yusuf is probably the closest to a complete narrative revealed in one complete *sura*. As a result, I have organized the prophets' stories in the order in which they occurred chronologically and historically. Because of the way the world has changed and the fact that humans are more easily engaged in continuity and structure, reading stories that have a beginning, middle, and end becomes more meaningful and significant in time and space. The stories of the prophets give a whole new meaning to the word *peace* that essentially sheds light on one's knowledge of Islam's magnificence and how its harmonious nature lies in the accounts of its messengers. God chose His prophets to reveal that He is the Creator of all things and that to Him we shall return. By believing in the revelations of the prophets, we find that our perception of the world changes, and our lives become colored by spiritual intensity and harmony. Our acceptance of life and death becomes intertwined in the mystical force of God the Creator, and His presence becomes no longer questionable.

By no means is this book a replacement for the reading of the stories of the prophets in context. Rather, it is written to inspire the reluctant reader to read about the prophets in the Qur'an more willingly, since their stories are cited sporadically in the Qur'an, but gathered in chapters in this manuscript. Also, readers must not despair at ambiguity or complex verses without reference to the Qur'an and Qur'anic exegesis when needed. This will help to reinforce the understanding of Islam's prophets, their messages of peace, and the belief in God and the Day of Judgment. It is crucial to note that many verses that reveal the stories of the prophets in the Qur'an were revealed to Prophet Muhammad *(pbuh)* over a period of twenty years and were reinforced through God's use of repetition. As a result, and to simplify the reading, repeated verses have been eliminated so that the reader may focus on the overall harmony of each story.

Subsequently, this text will not only serve as an examination of the stories of the prophets and their call for peace, but may also strengthen the reader's belief in the phenomenon of God in the absence of absolute proof and pacify the inner consciousness with a rationality that gradually embraces the mind and paves the way to a more concentrated faith.

Chapter 1

Prophet Adam—*Adam*

Theologians, philosophers, and commentators alike have been baffled throughout history over the mystery of creation and have, in one form or another, posited that those of us in search of a scientific confirmation of God's existence may never be satisfied. Take for example, "Pascal's wager" and the use of his concept of infinity. Even with his theory recommending that we choose from an "infinity of chances" to attain infinite happiness, time seems to be of the essence. It may appear to us that time is racing against all logic into the realm of infinity, but in reality, it will appear to come to a halt on the Final Day of Judgment as theistic evidence in the minds of believers, and with some degree of uncertainty in the minds of scientists and philosophers. In other words, there will be nothing to wait for. Time will become intertwined with one's final and eternal destiny.

It is also important to note that adherents of monotheistic religions have combined their philosophic and religious views by bonding man's existence with time and eternity. While on earth, man lives in a structured temporary frame of time and waits for an eternal time to reveal itself on the Day of Judgment. This concept of time is also a feature of the theology of St. Augustine (354–430 CE), the first major and perhaps one of the most influential religious philosophers who made a distinction in time between the period before Creation and the period afterwards. It did not appear that time prior to man eating of the tree was the same as time afterwards. It is only after man was told to fend for himself did time, an "ever-fixed eternity," become substituted with a predestined existence of temporary time.

This temporary frame of time began on the day the Prophet Adam began his life on earth and will return to its original form on the Day of Judgment.

> We (Allah) said: "O Prophet Adam!" "Dwell thou and thy wife in the garden and eat of the bountiful things therein as (where and when) ye will but approach not this tree or ye run into harm and transgression."[1] But Satan whispered evil to him: he said, "O Adam!" "Shall I lead thee to the Tree of Eternity and to a kingdom that never decays?" In the result they both ate of the tree and so their nakedness appeared to them: they began to sew together for their covering leaves from the Garden: thus did Adam disobey His Lord and allow himself to be seduced.[2]

Thus, in a fervent philosophical sense, and as prisoners of a so-called defined time, we hope that in the end we will be saved. To be saved, we must believe in God Almighty and pray that He extends His grace by awarding us the ability to carry out good deeds through peace and unification and thrust aside all temptations of evil. The Prophet Adam and his wife Eve were the sovereigns of peace and happiness, until they ate of the tree and fell from the garden of happiness into a world of predestined yet undefined time. By the same token, God's promise of eternal bliss or torment will give way to the confirmation of the aura of His transcendence in that He is beyond the universe and outside of time.

The Creation of Prophet Adam

> Say: "Is it that ye Deny Him Who created the earth in two Days?" "And do ye join equals with Him?" He is the Lord of (all) the Worlds.[3] We created the heavens and the earth and all between them in Six Days nor did any sense of weariness touch Us.[4] He

He said: "Your Lord only forbade you this tree lest ye should become angels or such beings as live for ever." And he swore to them both that he was their sincere adviser.[31] Then did Iblis make them slip from the (garden) and get them out of the state (of felicity) in which they had been.

We said: "Get ye down all (ye people) with enmity between yourselves. Earth will be your dwelling place and your means of livelihood for a time."[32]

We had already beforehand taken the covenant of Adam but he forgot: and We found on his part no firm resolve.

When We said to the angels: "Prostrate yourselves to Adam;" they prostrated but not Satan: he refused.

Then We said: "O Adam!" "Verily this is an enemy to thee and thy wife: so let him not get you both out of the Garden so that thou art landed in misery." "There is therein (enough provision) for thee not to go hungry nor to go naked; nor to suffer from thirst nor from the sun's heat." "But Iblis whispered evil to him."

He (Iblis) said: "...O Adam!" "Shall I lead thee to the Tree of Eternity and to a kingdom that never decays?" In the result they both ate of the tree and so their nakedness appeared to them: they began to sew together for their covering leaves from the Garden: thus did Adam disobey His Lord and allow himself to be seduced.[33]

The word "disobey" in this context may refer to the previous notion that Prophet Adam "forgot" to obey his Lord and was ultimately forgiven.

... And their Lord called unto them: "Did I not forbid you that tree and tell you that Satan was an avowed enemy unto you?"

They said: "Our Lord!" "We have wronged our own souls: if Thou forgive us not and bestow not upon us Thy mercy we shall certainly be lost."

Allah said: "Get ye down with enmity between yourselves." On earth will be your dwelling-place and your means of livelihood for a time." "… Therein shall ye live and therein shall ye die; but from it shall ye be taken out (at last)."[34]

Then learnt Adam from his Lord words of inspiration and his Lord turned toward him; for He is Oft-Returning Most Merciful.

We said: "Get ye down all from here; and if as is sure there comes to you guidance from Me whosoever follows My guidance, on them shall be no fear nor shall they grieve." "But those who reject Faith and believe in Our Signs, they shall be Companions of the Fire; they shall abide therein."[35]

O ye children of Adam! We have bestowed raiment upon you to cover your shame as well as to be an adornment to you but the raiment of righteousness that is the best. Such are among the signs of Allah that they may receive admonition or warning!

O ye children of Adam! Let not Satan seduce you in the same manner as he got your parents out of the garden stripping them of their raiment to expose their shame: for he and his tribe watch you from a position where ye cannot see them: We made the evil ones friends (only) to those without faith.[36]

O ye children of Adam! When ever there come to you apostles from amongst you rehearsing my signs unto you those who are righteous and mend (their lives,) on them shall be no fear nor shall they grieve.[37]

Your guardian-Lord is Allah Who created the heavens and the earth in six days and is firmly established on the throne (of authority): He draweth the night as a veil O'er the day, each seeking the other in rapid succession: He created the sun, the moon and the stars (all) governed by laws under His command. Is it not His to create and to govern? Blessed be Allah the cherisher and sustainer of the worlds![38]

God reveals the story of Qabil (*Cain*) and Habil (*Abel*) and how when Cain, puffed up with arrogance and jealousy, killed his innocent brother Abel.

Allah Addresses Prophet Muhammad *(pbuh):* Recite to them the truth of the story of the two sons of Adam. Behold! They each presented a sacrifice (to Allah.) It was accepted from one, but not from the other.

Said the latter: "Be sure I will slay thee." "Surely," said the former, "(Allah) doth accept of the sacrifice of those who are righteous. "If thou dost stretch thy hand against me, to slay me, it is not for me to stretch my hand against thee to slay thee: for I do fear Allah, the cherisher of the worlds." For me, I intend to let thee draw on thyself my sin as well as thine, for thou wilt be among the companions of the fire, and that is the reward of those who do wrong."

The (selfish) soul of the other led him to the murder of his brother: he murdered him, and became (himself) one of the lost ones.

Cain murdered his brother and left him without burial. He was the first human to commit murder and did not know what to do with his brother's body.

Then Allah sent a raven, who scratched the ground, to show him how to hide the shame of his brother. "Woe is me!" said he; "Was I not even able to be as this raven, and to hide the shame of my brother?" Then he became full of regrets-[39]

God sent the raven, a black bird, to show Qabil what to do with the corpse. Qabil observed the bird and buried Habil the same way. He felt guilty and ashamed for not knowing what to do with his brother, but not for killing him.

On that account: We ordained for the Children of Israel that if any one slew a person - unless it be for murder or for spreading mischief in the land - it would be as if he slew the whole people: and if any one saved a life, it would be as if he saved the life of the whole people. Then although there came to them Our apostles with clear signs, yet, even after that, many of them continued to commit excesses in the land.[40]

O mankind! Reverence your Guardian-Lord Who created you from a single person, created of like nature his mate and from them twain scattered (like seeds) countless men and women; reverence Allah through Whom ye demand your mutual (rights) and (reverence) the wombs (that bore you): for Allah ever watches over you.[41] Verily your Lord is Allah Who created the heavens and the earth in six Days and is firmly established on the Throne (of authority) regulating and governing all things. No intercessor (can plead with Him) except after His leave (hath been obtained). This is Allah your Lord; Him therefore serve ye: will ye not receive admonition?[42] It is He Who made the sun to be a shining glory and the moon to be a light (of beauty) and measured out stages for her: that ye might know the number of years and the count (of time). Nowise did Allah create this but in truth and righteousness. Thus, doth He explain his Signs in detail for those who understand.[43]

He it is Who created the heavens and the earth in six Days and His Throne was over the Waters that He might try you which of you is best in conduct. But if thou wert to say to them "Ye shall indeed be raised up after death" and the Unbelievers would be sure to say, "This is nothing but obvious sorcery!" [44]

He has created the heavens and the earth for just ends: far is He above having the partners they ascribe to Him! He has created man from a sperm drop; and behold this same (man) becomes an open disputer![45]

And Allah did create you from dust; then from a sperm-drop; then He made you in pairs. And no female conceives or lays down (her load) but with His knowledge. Nor is a man long-lived granted length of days nor is a part cut off from his life but is in a Decree (ordained). All this is easy for Allah.[46]

He created you (all) from a single person: then created of like nature his mate; and He sent down for you eight head of cattle in pairs (domesticated cattle that are useful to man): He makes you in the wombs of your mothers in stages one after another in three veils of darkness (in the cumulative sense, this represents the membrane, the womb, and the hollow in which the womb is enclosed). Such is Allah your Lord and Cherisher: to Him belongs (all) Dominion. There is no Allah but He: then how are ye turned away (from your true Center)? [47]

It is He Who has created you from dust then from a sperm-drop then from a leech-like clot; then does He get you out (into the light) as a child: then lets you (grow and) reach your age of full strength; then lets you become old though of you there are some who die before; and lets you reach a Term appointed: in order that ye may learn wisdom.[48]

It is He Who has created man from water: then has He established relationships of lineage and marriage: for thy Lord has power (over all things).[49]

Verily We created Man from a drop of mingled sperm in order to try him: so We gave him (the gifts) of Hearing and Sight.[50] Now, let man but think from what he is created! He is created from a drop emitted proceeding from between the backbone and the ribs.[51]

It is Allah Who created you in a state of (helpless) weakness then gave (you) strength after weakness then after strength gave (you) weakness and a hoary head: He creates as He wills and it is He Who has all knowledge and power.[52]

O mankind! If ye have a doubt about the Resurrection (consider) that We created you out of dust then out of sperm then out of a leech-like clot then out a morsel of flesh partly formed and partly unformed in order that We may manifest (Our Power) to you; and We cause whom We will to rest in the wombs for an appointed term then do We bring you out as babes then (foster you) that ye may reach your age of full strength; and some of you are called to die and some are sent back to the feeblest old age so that they know nothing after having known (much). And (further) thou seest the earth barren and lifeless but when We pour down rain on it, it is stirred (to life) it swells and it puts forth every kind of beautiful growth (in pairs).[53]

That He did create in pairs male and female. From a seed when lodged (in its place).[54] And cattle He has created for you (men): from them ye derive warmth and numerous benefits and of their (meat) ye eat. And ye have a sense of pride and beauty in them as ye drive them home in the evening and as ye lead them forth to pasture in the morning. And they carry your heavy loads to lands that ye could not (otherwise) reach except with souls distressed: for your Lord is indeed Most Kind, Most Merciful. And (He has created) horses, mules, and donkeys for you to ride and use for show; and He has created (other) things of what ye have no knowledge. And unto Allah leads straight the Way but there are ways that turn aside: if Allah had willed He could have guided all of you. It is He Who sends down rain from the sky: from it ye drink and out of it (grows) the vegetation on which ye feed your cattle. With it He produces for you corn, olives, date, palms grapes and every kind of fruit: verily in this is a Sign for those who give thought. He has made subject to you the Night and the Day; the Sun and the Moon; and the Stars are in subjection by His Command: verily in this are Signs for men who are wise. And the things on this earth that He has multiplied in varying colors (and qualities): verily in this is a Sign for men who celebrate the praises of Allah (in gratitude).

It is He Who has made the sea subject that ye may eat thereof flesh that is fresh and tender and that ye may extract therefrom ornaments to wear; and thou seest the ships therein that plough the waves that ye may seek (thus) of the bounty of Allah and that ye may be grateful. And He has set up on the earth, mountains standing firm lest it should shake with you; and rivers and roads; that ye may guide yourselves. And marks and signposts; and by the stars (men) guide themselves. Is then He Who creates like one that creates not? Will ye not receive admonition? If ye would count up the favors of Allah never would ye be able to number them: for Allah is Oft-Forgiving, Most Merciful. And Allah doth know what ye conceal and what ye reveal. Those whom they invoke besides Allah create nothing and are themselves created. (They are things) dead lifeless: nor do they know when they will be raised up.[55]

And verily in cattle (too) will ye find an instructive Sign. From what is within their bodies between excretions and blood We produce for your drink milk pure and agreeable to those who drink it. And from the fruit of the date-palm and the vine ye get out wholesome drink and food: behold in this also is a Sign for those who are wise. And thy Lord taught the Bee to build its cells in hills on trees and in (men's) habitations; Then to eat of all the produce (of the earth) and find with skill the spacious paths of its Lord: there issues from within their bodies a drink of varying colors wherein is healing for men: verily in this is a Sign for those who give thought.

It is Allah who creates you and takes your souls at death; and of you there are some who are sent back to a feeble age so that they know nothing after having known (much): for Allah is All-

Knowing All-Powerful. And Allah has made for you mates (and companions) of your own nature. And made for you out of them sons and daughters and grandchildren and provided for you sustenance of the best: will they then believe in vain things and be ungrateful for Allah's favors? And worship others than Allah such as have no power of providing them for sustenance with anything in heavens or earth and cannot possibly have such power?

Invent not similitude for Allah: for Allah knoweth and ye know not. To Allah belongeth the mystery of the heavens and the earth. And the decision of the Hour (of Judgment) is as the twinkling of an eye or even quicker: for Allah hath power over all things. It is He Who brought you forth from the wombs of your mothers when ye knew nothing; and He gave you hearing and sight and intelligence and affections: that ye may give thanks (to Allah). Do they not look at the birds held poised in the midst of (the air and) the sky? Nothing holds them up but (the power of) Allah. Verily in this are Signs for those who believe.

It is Allah who made your habitations homes of rest and quiet for you; and made for you out of the skins of animals (tents for) dwellings which ye find so light (and handy) when ye travel and when ye stop (in your travels); and out of their wool and their soft fibers (between wool and hair) and their hair rich stuff and articles of convenience (to serve you) for a time. It is Allah who made out of the things He created some things to give you shade; of the hills He made some for your shelter; He made you garments to protect you from heat and coats of mail to protect you from your (mutual) violence. Thus does He complete his favors on you that ye may bow to His will (in Islam).[56]

The number of months in the sight of Allah is twelve (in a year) so ordained by Him the day He created the heavens and the earth; of them four are sacred (Zul-qa'd, Zul-haj, Muharram, and Rajab are the months in which Allah forbids fighting); that is the straight usage. So wrong not yourselves therein and fight the pagans all together as they fight you all together. The pagan Arabs changed the four sacred months about in order to fight when their enemy least expected it. But know that Allah is with those who restrain themselves.[57]

Your Lord is He that maketh the Ship go smoothly for you through the sea in order that ye may seek of His Bounty: for He is unto you Most Merciful.[58] We have honored the sons of Prophet Adam; provided them with transport on land and sea; given them for sustenance things good and pure; and conferred on them special favors above a great part of Our Creation.[59]

This is so because Allah is the Reality: it is He Who gives life to the dead and it is He Who has power over all things.[60] Those who believe (in the Qur'an) those who follow the Jewish (scriptures) and the Sabians, Christians, Magians and Polytheists.

Thus, the Magians were a very ancient cult. Their location was the Persian and Median uplands and the Mespotamian valleys. They are the Wise Men of the East who were also mentioned in the Gospels.

Allah will judge between them on the Day of Judgment: for Allah is witness of all things.[61] And no question do they bring to thee but We reveal to thee the truth and the best explanation (thereof.). [62]

We have enjoined on man to be kind to his parents for in pain did his mother bear him and in pain did she give him birth. The carrying of the (child) to his weaning is (a period of) thirty months.

Women usually breast-fed their children for a period of thirty months or until a child reached two and a half years of age.

At length when he reaches the age of full strength and attains forty years he says "O my Lord!" "Grant me that I may be grateful for Thy favor which Thou hast bestowed upon me and upon both my parents and that I may work righteousness such as Thou mayest approve; and be gracious to me in my issue." "Truly have I turned to Thee and truly do I bow (to Thee) in Islam." [63]

Generally, man grows and matures spiritually by the age of forty and turns to God for forgiveness and guidance. By then, his worldly desires become less appealing than his perception of life in the hereafter.

O mankind! We created you from a single (pair) of a male and a female and made you into nations and tribes that ye may know each other (not that ye may despise each other). Verily the most honored of you in the sight of Allah is (he who is) the most righteous of you. And Allah has full knowledge and is well acquainted (with all things). [64]

(Allah) Most Gracious! It is He Who has taught the Qur'an. He has created man: He has taught him speech (and Intelligence). The sun and the moon follow courses (exactly) computed.

Scientists today have established exact mathematical laws that predict the revolution of the earth around the sun. This sentence appeals to those in search of scientific evidence of the authenticity of the Qur'an.

… And the herbs and the trees—both (alike) bow in adoration. And the Firmament (sky) has He raised high and He has set up the balance (of Justice). In order that ye may not transgress (due) balance. [65] He created man from sounding clay like unto pottery. And He created *Jinn*s from fire free of smoke: [66] That it is He who Granteth Laughter and Tears; That it is He who Granteth Death and Life; [67] (He is) Lord of the two Easts and Lord of the two Wests: [68] He has let free the two bodies of flowing water meeting together. Between them is a Barrier which they do not transgress: [69] It is We Who have created you: why will ye not witness the Truth? Do ye then see? The (human seed) that ye throw out. Is it ye who create it or are We the Creators? [70]

Here, the two Easts (Southeast and Northeast) are "the two extreme points where the sun rises during the year and includes all the points in between. Similarly, the two Wests (Southwest and Northwest) include the two extreme points of the sun's setting and all the points in between."[71]

> Does Man think that he will be left uncontrolled (without purpose)? Was he not a drop of sperm emitted (in lowly form)? Then did he become a leech-like clot; then did (Allah) make and fashion (him) in due proportion. And of him He made two sexes male and female. Has not He (the same) the power to give life to the dead?[72]

God's words and fundamental proposal through each of His prophets was to endow peace and justice on earth. The Qur'an's stories adequately describe the thorny trail originally embarked on by the Prophet Adam and by Eve and God's willingness to forgive them and all of their descendents if they believe in His Oneness and the hereafter and are willing to live peacefully with one another. Those who continue to follow Iblis's course to create war and mischief on earth will be given their ruling on the Day of Judgment.

Chapter 2

Prophet Idris —*Enoch*

The Prophet Idris is mentioned twice in the Qur'an and was known to be wise, judicious, patient, and determined. He was born in Babylon and was the fifth generation of the Prophet Adam and his son Seth. He called upon his people to live in peace and follow the religion of his forefathers. He was often ridiculed and found himself driven to migrate to Egypt. He left Babylon and went to Egypt to expand his teachings and gain more supporters. He taught people to believe in God, pray, fast, and give to the poor, and was presumably the first to invent the basic form of writing. God has praised the Prophet Idris, describing him as being a prophet and truthful:

> And (remember) Isma'il, Idrís, and Zul-kifl, all (men) of constancy and patience.[1]

> Also mention in the Book the case of Idris: He was a man of truth (and sincerity), (and) a prophet: And We raised him to a lofty station. [2]

Given that, as stated earlier, the focal point of this book is to relate the stories of the prophets found in the Qur'an, I have sparingly used

Qur'anic exegesis in order to reduce any partiality and give the reader a chance to make his/her own analysis of the stories of the prophets as they are cited in the Qur'an. However, since very little is known about the Prophet Idris, I have chosen to share one of the many stories that were written about him by various Islamic preachers and authors.

According to Abu Ja'far, Imam Muhammad Al-Baqir, there was a tyrannical king who coveted the land of one of the Prophet Idris's followers. He offered to purchase the property, but its owner refused to sell it to him in order to be able to provide for his family. When the king informed his wife of this, she suggested that he accuse the man of blasphemy, kill him, and possess the land. The king complied with his wife's request, killed the man, and ruthlessly left the poor man's wife and children to fend for themselves. [3]

God inspired the Prophet Idris to inform the king and his wife that he was going to avenge the killing of one of his innocent followers. The king was alarmed and vowed to kill the Prophet Idris by sending a herd of men after him, but the Prophet Idris was out of sight. Eventually, God stripped the tyrant of his authority and reduced his kingdom to ruins.[4]

In the end, the Prophet Idris spent many years advising his people to live in peace and to be humble. He urged those who were in search of monetary wealth to seek spiritual wealth instead. By teaching his people to believe in God and live peacefully among each other, he was able to carry out his purpose and spend the rest of his life praising the Almighty.

Chapter 3

Prophet Nuh— *Noah*

Prior to the arrival of the Prophet Nuh, people were corrupt. Most of them did not think of God and were vicious and immoral. People worshipped and served Gods of their own making and became followers of evil and transgression. Once again, God saw the need to remind people that this world was only temporary and that eventually they will face Him and be judged for their actions. The Prophet Nuh was chosen to help promote the belief in God while establishing stability, peace, and virtue among his people.

The Prophet Nuh was a man of "humility, gentleness, firmness, persuasiveness, truth, and love for his own people."[1] The Qur'an states that the Prophet Nuh lived for a thousand minus fifty years; however, this has been interpreted in different ways by traditional scholarly exegesis, and there is some disagreement about his real age from the time he was chosen to be prophet to the time of his death. The nine hundred and fifty years could have been prior to the hurricane or flood, and he may have lived many years beyond that. Nonetheless, there is consensus that the Prophet Nuh began his prophecy one thousand years after the Prophet Adam.[2] Even though he was a very wise and tolerant man; his people were stubborn and chose to reject his prophecy and the willingness to believe in one

God. He tried for many years to enlighten them and remind them of life in the hereafter, but they were engaged in sin and had no respect for his warnings. God decided to save those who yearned to believe in Him and drown the nonbelievers in a flood. The Prophet Nuh was directed by God to build an Ark so that he might save the righteous.[3]

We sent Noah to his people and he tarried among them a thousand years less fifty: but the Deluge overwhelmed them while they (persisted in) sin.[4]

Noah said: "...O my people!" "Worship Allah!" "Ye have no other Allah but Him: will ye not fear (Him)?"

Chief of the unbelievers said: "...He is no more than a man like yourselves: his wish is to assert his superiority over you: if Allah had wished (to send messengers) He could have sent down angels: never did we hear such a thing (as he says) among our ancestors of old."

And some said: "He is only a man possessed: have patience and give him time."[5]

Noah said: "I have come to you with a Clear Warning: That ye serve none but Allah: verily I do fear for you the Penalty of a Grievous Day."

But the Chief of the unbelievers among his people said: "We see (in) thee nothing but a man like ourselves: nor do we see that any follow thee but the meanest among us in judgment immature: nor do we see in you (all) any merit above us: in fact we think ye are liars!"

Noah said: "O my people!" "See ye if (it be that) I have a Clear

Sign from my Lord and that He hath sent Mercy unto me from His own Presence but that the Mercy hath been obscured from your sight?" "Shall we compel you to accept it when ye are averse to it?" "And O my People!" "I ask you for no wealth in return: my reward is from none but Allah: but I will not drive away (in contempt) those who believe: for verily they are to meet their Lord and ye I see are the ignorant ones!" "And O my People!" "Who would help me against Allah if I drove them away?" "Will ye not then take heed?" "I tell you not that with me are the Treasures of Allah nor do I know what is hidden nor claim I to be an angel. Nor yet do I say of those whom your eyes do despise that Allah will not grant them (all) that is good: Allah knoweth best what is in their souls: I should if I did indeed be a wrongdoer."

They said: "O Noah!" "Thou hast disputed with us and (much) hast thou prolonged the dispute with us: now bring upon us what thou threatenest us with if thou speakest the truth!"

Noah said: "Truly Allah will bring it on you if He wills and then ye will not be able to frustrate it!" "Of no profit will be my counsel to you much as I desire to give you (good) counsel if it be that Allah willeth to leave you astray: He is your Lord and to Him will ye return!"

Allah revealed: Or do they say "He has forged it?" Say: "If I forged it on me is my sin!" "And I am free of the sins of which ye are guilty!"[6] "...If it be hard on your (mind) that I should stay (with you) and commemorate the Signs of Allah yet I put my trust in Allah." "Get ye then an agreement about your plan and among your partners so your plan be not to you dark and dubious." "Then pass your sentence on me and give me no respite." "But if ye turn back (consider): no reward have I asked of you: my reward is only due from Allah and I have been commanded to be of those who submit to Allah's Will (in Islam)."[7] "...O my people!" "Worship Allah!" "Ye have no other Allah but Him." "I fear for you the punishment of a dreadful day!"

The leaders of his people said: "Ah!" "We see thee evidently wandering (in mind)."

Noah said: "O my people!" "No wandering is there in my (mind): on the contrary I am an apostle from the Lord and Cherisher of the worlds!" "I but fulfill towards you the duties of my Lord's mission: sincere is my advice to you and I know from Allah something that ye know not." "Do ye wonder that there hath come to you a message from your Lord through a man of your own people to warn you so that ye may fear Allah and haply receive his mercy?"[8] The people of Noah rejected the apostles. "Will ye not fear (Allah)?" "I am to you an apostle worthy of all trust: So fear Allah and obey me." "No reward do I ask of you for it: my reward is only from the Lord of the Worlds: So fear Allah and obey me."

They said: "Shall we believe in thee when it is the meanest that follow thee?"

Noah said: "And what do I know as to what they do?" "Their account is only with my Lord if ye could (but) understand." "I am not one to drive away those who believe." "I am sent only to warn plainly in public."

They said: "If thou desist not O Noah!" "Thou shalt be stoned (to death)."

Noah said: "O my Lord!" "Truly my people have rejected me. Judge thou then between me and them openly and deliver me and those of the Believers who are with me."[9]

Allah revealed: "…Do thou warn thy people before there comes to them a grievous Penalty."

Noah said: "O my People!" "I am to you a Warner clear and open: That ye should worship Allah fear Him and obey me so He may forgive you your sins and give you respite for a stated Term: For when the Term given by Allah is accomplished it cannot be put forward: if ye only knew."

Noah appealed to Allah: "...O my Lord!" "I have called to my People night and day: But my call only increases (their) flight (from the Right). And every time I have called to them that Thou mightest forgive them they have (only) thrust their fingers into their ears covered themselves up with their garments grown obstinate and given themselves up to arrogance. So I have called to them aloud." "Further I have spoken to them in public and secretly in private saying", "Ask forgiveness from your Lord; for He is Oft-Forgiving; He will send rain to you in abundance; give you increase in wealth and sons; and bestow on you gardens and bestow on you rivers (of flowing water)."

Allah revealed: "What is the matter with you that ye place not your hope for kindness and long-suffering in Allah seeing that it is He that has created you in diverse stages?" "See ye not how Allah has created the seven heavens one above another and made the moon a light in their midst and made the sun as a (glorious) lamp?" "And Allah has produced you from the earth growing (gradually) And in the End, He will return you into the (earth) and raise you forth (again at the Resurrection); And Allah has made the earth for you as a carpet (spread out) that ye may go about therein in spacious roads."

Noah appealed to Allah: "...O my Lord!" "They have disobeyed me but they follow (men) whose wealth and children give them no increase but only loss; and they have devised a tremendous plot." "And they have said (to each other) abandon not your gods; abandon neither Wadd nor Suwa neither Yaguth nor Ya'uq nor Nasr'. All of the gods they worshipped were given names. They have already misled many; and grant Thou no increase to the wrongdoers but in straying from their mark." ... "O my Lord!"

"Leave not of the Unbelievers a single one on earth!" "For if Thou dost leave (any of) them they will but mislead thy devotees and they will breed none but wicked ungrateful ones." "Oh my Lord, forgive me my parents all who enter my house in Faith and (all) believing men and believing women: and to the wrongdoers grant Thou no increase but in Perdition!"[10]

Allah revealed: "…None of thy people will believe except those who have believed already!" "So grieve no longer over their (evil) deeds."[11]

The Prophet Noah is pleading with God to let the unbelievers go astray before they mislead more people. His people did not want to believe in God nor did they want to believe that it would be possible for them to die and be raised again. To them, the only life was the life they were living.

"He is only a man who invents a lie against Allah but we are not the ones to believe in him!"[12]

"…Construct the Ark within Our sight and under Our guidance: then when comes Our command and the fountains of the earth gush forth take thou on board pairs of every species male and female and thy family except those of them against whom the Word has already gone forth: and address Me not in favor of the wrongdoers; for they shall be drowned (in the Flood)." And when thou hast embarked on the Ark thou and those with thee say, "Praise be to Allah Who has saved us from the people who do wrong." And say, "O my Lord!" "Enable me to disembark with Thy blessing: for Thou art the Best to enable (us) to disembark."[13] Forthwith he starts constructing the Ark: every time that the Chiefs of his People passed by him they threw ridicule on him.

Noah said: "…If ye ridicule us now we (in our turn) can look down on you with ridicule likewise!" But soon will ye know who it is on whom will descend a Penalty that will cover them with shame will be unloosed a Penalty lasting.

Allah revealed: "...Embark therein of each kind two male and female and your family except those against whom the Word has already gone forth and the Believers." But only a few believed with him.

Noah said: "Embark ye on the Ark in the name of Allah whether it move or be at rest!" "For my Lord is surely, Oft-Forgiving Most Merciful!"[14]

The Prophet Nuh is mentioned in the Qur'an as being one of the five greatest prophets. He was respectful and dedicated to believing in God. In Islam people are judged by their actions. That is, if a man professes belief in Islam and performs the religious duties of primary importance, he is treated as a believer by God. The Prophet Nuh was not aware that his son was not a believer until the day he ordered his people to board the Ark. When his son refused to embark, stating that God would not be able to drown him since he would stand on the highest of mountains, the Prophet Nuh prayed that God might forgive him.

Noah called upon Allah and said: "O my Lord!" "Surely my son is of my family" and Thy promise is true and Thou art the Justest of Judges!"

Allah revealed: "O Noah!" "He is not of thy family: for his conduct is unrighteous." "So ask not of Me that of which thou hast no knowledge!" "I give thee counsel lest thou act like the ignorant!"

Noah said: "O my Lord!" "I do seek refuge with Thee lest I ask Thee for that of which I have no knowledge." "And unless Thou forgive me and have Mercy on me I should indeed be lost!"[15] "...I am one overcome: do Thou then help (me)?"

So We opened the gates of heaven with water pouring forth. And We caused the earth to gush forth with springs so the waters met (and rose) to the extent decreed. But We bore him on an (Ark) made of broad planks and caulked with palm-fiber: She floats under Our eyes (and care): a recompense to one who had been rejected (with scorn)![16] So the Ark floated with them on the waves (towering) like mountains ...

Noah called out to his son who had separated himself (from the rest): "O my son!" "Embark with us and be not with the Unbelievers!"

The son replied: "I will take myself to some mountain: it will save me from the water."

Noah said: "This day nothing can save from the Command of Allah any but those on whom He hath mercy!" And the waves came between them and the son was among those overwhelmed in the Flood. When the word went forth: "O earth!" "Swallow up thy water and O sky!" "Withhold (thy rain)!" And the water abated and the matter was ended. The Ark rested on Mount Judi and the word went forth: "Away with those who do wrong!"[17] And We have left this as a Sign (for all time): then is there any that will receive admonition?[18]

(In the days of old), Noah cried to Us and We are the Best to hear prayer.[19] Because of their sins they were drowned (in the flood) and were made to enter the Fire (of Punishment); and they found in lieu of Allah none to help them.[20] And We delivered him and his people from the Great Calamity. And made his progeny to endure (on this earth); And We left (this blessing) for him among generations to come in later time. Peace and salutation to Prophet Noah among the nations! Thus indeed do We reward those who do right. For he was one of Our believing Servants.[21] But they rejected him, and We delivered him and those with him in the ark: But We overwhelmed in the flood those who rejected our signs. They were indeed a blind people![22] ...Then see what was the end of those who were warned but heeded not![23]

The word came: "O Noah!" "Come down (from the Ark) with Peace from Us and Blessings on thee and on some of the Peoples (who will spring) from those with thee: but (there will be other) Peoples to whom We shall grant their pleasures (for a time) but in the end will a grievous Penalty reach them from Us."[24]

Allah appeals to mankind: "...O ye that are sprung from those whom We carried (in the Ark) with Noah!" Verily he was a devotee most grateful.[25] How many generations have We destroyed after Noah? And enough is thy Lord to note and see the sins of His servants.[26] Such are some of the stories of the Unseen, which We have revealed unto thee: before this neither thou nor thy People knew them. So persevere patiently: for the End is for those who are righteous.[27] And the people of Noah when they rejected the apostles We drowned them and We made them as a Sign for mankind; and We have prepared for (all) wrongdoers a grievous Penalty.[28]

Allah sets forth for an example to the Unbelievers the wife of Noah and the wife of Lut: they were (respectively) under two of Our righteous servants but they were false to their (husbands) and they profited nothing before Allah on their account but were told: "Enter ye the fire along with (others) that enter!"[29]

But (there were people) before them who denied (the Signs) the People of Noah and the confederates (of Evil) after them; and every People plotted against their prophet to seize him and disputed by means of vanities therewith to condemn the truth; but it was I that seized them! And how (terrible) was My Requital! Thus was the Decree of thy Lord proved true against the Unbelievers; that truly they are Companions of Fire![30]

Verily in this there are Signs (for men to understand); (thus) do We try (men). Prophet Noah was not the first or last of prophets. Allah sent many prophets after him who were ridiculed and disrespected. Then We raised after them another generation; And We sent to them an apostle from among themselves (saying) "Worship Allah!" "You have no other Allah but Him. Will ye not fear (Him)?" And the chiefs of his people who disbelieved and denied the Meeting in the Hereafter and on whom We had bestowed the good things of this life said: "He is no more than a man like yourselves; he eats of that of which ye eat and drinks of what ye drink." "If ye obey a man like yourselves behold it is certain ye will be lost." "Does he promise that when ye die and become dust and bones ye shall be brought forth (again)?"[31]

Allah revealed: In but a little while they are sure to be sorry! Then the Blast overtook them with justice and We made them as rubbish of dead leaves floating on the stream of Time! So away with the people who do wrong![32]

When the Prophet Nuh finally reached land and God ordered him to leave the Ark so that He might grant him peace and blessings, the message was clear that God valued mankind and wanted His prophet, and those who joined him on his life-threatening journey, to live in the newly liberated world of peace. Peace, in this sense, is a by-product of devotion and contentment, and it could only exist if the Prophet Nuh and his people were willing to center their lives on trying to reach an ideal world and believe in Islam and the Oneness of God.

Chapter 4

Prophet Hud

The Prophet Hud tried repeatedly to exhort the South Arabian people (the Ad) to believe in Islam and worship One God, but they refused. The Qur'an states that their disbelief was punished by a decimating "sterilizing wind" (*ar-rih al-aqim*). While some traditions support the etymological identification of the Prophet Hud with the biblical Heber, other accounts represent him as a southern Arabian merchant. Several sites are revered as the Prophet Hud's tomb, the most notable being in Yemen, but that are other theories that reveal he was buried in Najaf, Iraq. The Prophet Hud is also linked to monuments in Mecca and Damascus.

With more corruption and lack of faith in the Divine, God inspired the Prophet Hud to alert His creation to fear the penalty of the Great Day and to worship Him. The story of the Prophet Hud appears to display similarities between how he was treated by his people and how Prophet Muhammad *(pbuh)* was treated by the Meccans. The Ad people, as did the Meccans, adhered to false gods even after they were informed of the true God.[1] In addition, the wealthy suppressed the poor. Thus, the Prophet Hud informed them that unless they believed in God and treated the poor justly, there would never be peace among them. He stressed that they would be subject to God's wrath not only in this world, but in the hereafter as well.

Remember also the Ad and the Thamud (people): clearly will appear to you from (the traces) of their buildings (their fate): the Evil One made their deeds alluring to them and kept them back from the Path though they were gifted with Intelligence and Skill.[2] ... We sent Prophet Hud one of their own brethren.

Hud said: "...O my people!" "Worship Allah!" "Ye have no other Allah but Him." "You do nothing but invent your other gods!"[3] "...Will ye not fear (Allah)?" "I am to you an apostle worthy of all trust." "So fear Allah and obey me." "No reward do I ask of you for it: my reward is only from the Lord of the Worlds." "Do ye build a landmark on every high place to amuse yourselves?" "And do ye get for yourselves fine buildings in the hope of living therein (forever)?" "And when ye exert your strong hand do ye do it like men of absolute power?" "Now fear Allah and obey me." "Yea fear Him Who has bestowed on you freely all that ye know." "Freely has He bestowed on you cattle and sons and gardens and springs." "Truly I fear for you the Penalty of a Great Day."[4]

The Ad people were very arrogant and ignored the Prophet Hud's warnings.

They said: "It is the same to us whether thou admonish us or be not among (our) Admonishers!" "This is no other than a customary device of the ancients." "And we are not the ones to receive Pains and Penalties!" [5]

Hud said: "...O my people!" "I ask of you no reward for this (Message)." "My reward is from none but Him Who created me: will ye not then understand?" "And O my people!" "Ask forgiveness of your Lord and turn to Him (in repentance): He will send you the skies pouring abundant rain and add strength to your strength: so turn ye not back in sin!"[6] "...O my people!" "I am no imbecile but (I am) an apostle from the Lord and Cherisher of the worlds!" "I am fulfilling the duties of my Lord's mission: I am to you a sincere and trustworthy adviser." "Do ye wonder that there hath come to you a message from your Lord through a man of your own people to warn you?" "Call in remembrance that he made you inheritors after the people of Prophet Noah and gave you a stature tall among the nations." "Call in remembrance the benefits (ye have received) from Allah: that so Ye may prosper."

They said: "Comest thou to us that we may worship Allah alone and give up the cult of our fathers?" "Bring us what thou threatenest us with if so be that thou tellest the truth!"

Hud said: "Punishment and wrath have already come upon you from your Lord: dispute ye with me over names which ye and your fathers have devised without authority from Allah?" "Then wait, I am amongst you also waiting."[7]

They said: "O Prophet Hud!" "No Clear (Sign) hast thou brought us and we are not the ones to desert our gods on thy word!" "Nor do we believe in thee!" "We say nothing but that (perhaps) some of our gods may have seized thee with imbecility."

Hud said: "I call Allah to witness and do ye bear witness that I am free from the sin of ascribing to Him other gods as partners!" "So scheme (your worst) against me all of you and give me no respite." "I put my trust in Allah my Lord and your Lord!" "There is not a moving creature but He hath grasp of its forelock." "Verily it is my Lord that is on a Straight Path." "If ye turn away I (at least) have conveyed the Message with which I was sent to you." "My Lord will make another People to succeed you and you will not harm Him in the least." "For my Lord hath care and watch over all things."[8]

They said: "Hast thou come in order to turn us aside from Our gods?" "Then bring upon us the (calamity) with which thou dost threaten us if thou art telling the truth!"

Hud said: "The Knowledge (of when it will come) is only with Allah: I proclaim to you the mission on which I have been sent: but I see that ye are a people in ignorance!"[9]

Now the 'Ad behaved arrogantly through the land, against (all) truth and reason, and said: "Who is superior to us in strength?" "What!" "Did they not see that Allah Who created them was superior to them in strength?"

But they continued to reject Our Signs! So We sent against them a furious Wind through days of disaster that We might give them a taste of a Penalty of humiliation in this Life; but the Penalty of the Hereafter will be more humiliating still: and they will find no help.[10]

Then when they saw the (Penalty in the shape of) a cloud traversing the sky coming to meet their valleys ...

They said: "This cloud will give us rain!"

Nay, it is the (calamity) ye were asking to be hastened! A wind wherein is a Grievous Penalty! Everything will it destroy by the command of its Lord! Then by the morning they - nothing was to be seen but (the ruins of) their houses! Thus do We recompense those given to sin![11] Plucking out men as if they were roots of palm-trees torn up (from the ground).[12] It left nothing whatever that it came up against but reduced it to ruin and rottenness.[13] We saved him and those who adhered to him by our mercy and We cut off the roots of those who rejected our signs and did not believe.[14]

The Prophet Hud tried very hard to educate his people and inform them that by worshipping idols they were misleading themselves and would be doomed on the Day of Judgment. His sincerity and trustworthiness raised him above the ignorant and arrogant people of his time and away from God's wrath and the calamity of the gusty winds. God saved the Prophet Hud and those who adhered to his beliefs so that he might continue to spread peace and humility among his people.

Chapter 5

Prophet Salih

The Prophet Salih, a descendant of the Thamud people, lived in *Hajar*, a town located between Syria and Hejaz. When the Prophet Salih's people became corrupt, God inspired him to urge his people to worship Him. They refused to submit to his request unless he could provide them with a miracle that would prove God's existence. They asked that God send them a woolly red she-camel. God complied with the Prophet Salih's request and directed him to inform his people that the she-camel was to share water with them on alternate days and that they were not allowed to do it any harm. As time went by, they outgrew their patience, disobeyed the Prophet Salih, and killed the camel. As a result, the Prophet Salih told them that God was going to avenge the camel's death. Within three days after the camel's death, God responded with a strike of lightning and the people were left lifeless in their homes.[1] Hence, their skill in building their homes was not enough for God to approve of them.

To the Thamud People (We sent) Prophet Salih one of their own brethren.

He said: "O my people! Worship Allah. Ye have no other god but Him. It is He Who hath produced you from the earth and settled you therein: then ask forgiveness of Him, and turn to Him (in repentance): for my Lord is (always) near, ready to answer."[2]

Behold their brother Salih said to them: "Will you fear (Allah)?" "I am to you an apostle worthy of all trust." "So fear Allah and obey me." "No reward do I ask of you for it: my reward is only from the Lord of the Worlds." "Will ye be left secure in (the enjoyment of) all that ye have here?—Gardens and Springs and corn-fields and date-palms with spathes near breaking (with the weight of fruit)?" "And ye carve house out of (rocky) mountains with great skill." "But fear Allah and obey me, and follow not the bidding of those who are extravagant—who make mischief in the land and mend not (their ways)."

The Thamud people said: "Thou art only of those bewitched!" "Thou art no more than a mortal like us: then bring us a Sign if thou tellest the truth!"[3]

Salih said: "...Serve Allah", but behold, they became two factions quarrelling with each other. "...O my people!" "Why ask you to hasten on the evil in preference to the good?" "If only ye ask Allah for forgiveness, ye may hope to receive mercy."

The Thamud people said: "Ill omen do we augur from thee and those that are with thee."

Salih said: "Your ill omen is with Allah; yea ye are a people under trial." There were in the City nine men of a family who made mischief in the land and would not reform.

The Thamud people said: "Swear a mutual oath by Allah that we shall make a secret night attack on him and his people and that we shall then say to his heir (when he seeks vengeance): We were not present at the slaughter of his people and we are positively telling the truth." They plotted and planned but We too planned even while they perceived it not.[4]

Salih said: "...O my people!" "Worship Allah: ye have no other Allah but Him." "It is He Who hath produced you from the earth and settled you therein: then ask forgiveness of Him and turn to Him (in repentance): for my Lord in (always) near ready to answer."

The Thamud people said: "O Salih!" "Thou hast been of us! A center of our hopes hitherto!" "Dost thou (now) forbid us the worship of what our fathers worshipped?" "But we are really in suspicious (disquieting) doubt as to that to which thou invitest us."

Salih said: "O my people!" "Do ye see?" "If I have a Clear (Sign) from my Lord and He hath sent Mercy unto me from Himself who then can help me against Allah if I were to disobey Him?" "What then would ye add to my (portion) but perdition?" "And O my people!" "This she-camel of Allah is a symbol to you: leave her to feed on Allah's (free) earth and inflict no harm on her or a swift Penalty will seize you!"[5] And tell them that the water is to be divided between them: each one's right to drink being brought forward (by suitable turns).[6] But they did hamstring her.

Salih said: "Enjoy yourselves in your homes for three days: (then will be your ruin): there is a promise not to be belied!"[7]

Salih left them saying: "...O my people!" "I did indeed convey to you the message for which I was sent by my Lord: I gave you good counsel but ye love not good counselors!"[8]

When Our Decree issued We saved Prophet Salih and those who believed with him by (special) Grace from Ourselves and from the Ignominy of that Day. For thy Lord He is the Strong One and Able to enforce His Will. The (mighty) Blast overtook the wrongdoers and they lay prostrate in their homes before the morning as if they had never dwelt and flourished there. Ah! Behold! For the Thamud rejected their Lord and Cherisher! Ah! Behold! Removed (from sight) were the Thamud!"[9] We sent them Our Signs but they persisted in turning away from them. Out of the mountains did they hew (their) edifices (feeling themselves) secure. But the (mighty) Blast seized them of a morning and of no avail to them was all that they did (with such art and care)![10]

And We refrain from sending the Signs only because the men of former generations treated them as false: We sent the She-camel: to the Thamud to open their eyes but they treated her wrongfully. We only send the Signs by way of terror (and warning from evil). Behold! We told thee that thy Lord doth encompass humankind round about. We granted the Vision which We showed thee but as a trial for men as also the Cursed Tree (mentioned) in the Qur'an. We put terror (and warning) into them but it only increases their inordinate transgression![11]

The Thamud people should have respected the Prophet Salih's request and created peace and harmony among themselves and submitted to God's will. Unfortunately, they were quite contemptuous, and peace could not be created at a state level where every man felt that his home was his castle. Judging from God's perspective, man should pursue one unified world of creation void of arrogance and tribal segregation.

Chapter 6

Prophet Ibrahim—*Abraham*

The Prophet Ibrahim was the first of the prophets who lived and died in Palestine. He is the ancestral father of Judaism, Christianity, and Islam. He was born in the city of Ur in the south of what is now modern Iraq and was buried in the city of Hebron in Palestine. After God delivered him from the persecution of his people, he migrated to Harran in northern Syria and then to the Land of Canaan (Palestine) around 1900 BCE.[1]

The story of the Prophet Ibrahim is the story of a man who was predestined to become a leader to all nations. God communicated with him through visions and angels disguised in the form of man. The Prophet Ibrahim was inspired to make great sacrifices for God's sake. In fact, his belief in the One and only God led him to stand against his own community, specifically his father who not only worshipped idols, but made them with his own hands. It is important to note that some schools of thought believe that Azar was the Prophet Ibrahim's stepfather and not his biological father. He will be referred to as his father from here on in order to comply with Yusuf Ali's translation.

The Prophet Ibrahim was thrown into the fire by the tyrant ruler Nemrud for having broken all the idols. Even though Nemrud believed that the Prophet Ibrahim's God must be powerful since the Prophet Ibrahim did not burn, he refused to let go of his creed. Eventually the Prophet Ibrahim's opposition led him to be the subject of legal repercussions and exile. His nephew Lut, along with a group of people who believed in his mission, migrated together in the cause of God. The Prophet Ibrahim's title became "the friend of God" and *haneef,* one who is upright. The mystery of creation and the existence of a power beyond the comprehension of man bewildered him. He felt at peace in his soul and wondered why his people couldn't connect with God and feel the same. He longed for a world of peace, a world transcending the world of consciousness, where people could value God's existence and creation. He spent his life serving God and in fact, was one of God's preferred prophets.

… Abraham was a man of Truth, a prophet.[2] … Abraham was tried by his Lord with certain commands which he fulfilled.

Allah revealed: "I will make thee an Imam to the nations."

Abraham said: "And also (Imams) from my offspring!"

Allah answered: "But my promise is not within the reach of evil-doers."[3]

We bestowed aforetime on Abraham his rectitude of conduct and well were We acquainted with him.[4]

Behold! His Lord said to him: "Bow (thy will to me)!"

Abraham said: "I bow (my will) to the Lord and Cherisher of the universe."[5]

The Prophet Ibrahim admired God's creation and the world around him. God gave him guidance from an early age. His observations and analysis of all that surrounded him confirmed that nothing other than a divine force could create such a mystifying universe. He hoped that the day would come when God would show him how to guide the nonbelievers. He wanted everyone to share in his belief and ultimately transmitted his aspirations to his father Azar.

So, also did We show Abraham the power and the laws of the heavens and the earth that he might (with understanding) have certitude. When the night covered him over he saw a star.

Abraham said: "This is my Lord, but when it set he said, I love not those that set." When he saw the moon rising in splendor, he said, "This is my Lord, but when the moon set he said, unless my Lord guide me I shall surely be among those who go astray." When he saw the sun rising in splendor he said, "This is my Lord; this is the greatest (of all)." But when the sun set he said, "O my people!" "I am (now) free from your (guilt) of giving partners to Allah. For me I have set my face firmly and truly toward Him Who created the heavens and the earth, and never shall I give partners to Allah."[6]

Lo! Abraham said to his father Azar: "Takest thou idols for gods? "Thee and thy people are in manifest error."[7]

His people disputed with him.

Abraham said: "(Come) ye to dispute with me about Allah when He (Himself) hath guided me?" "I fear not (the beings) ye associate with Allah: unless my Lord willeth (nothing can happen)." "My Lord comprehendeth in His knowledge all things: will ye not (yourselves) be admonished?" "How should I fear (the beings) ye associate with Allah when ye fear not to give partners to Allah without any warrant having been given to you?" "Which of (us) two parties hath more right to security?" "Tell me if ye know."[8]

Abraham said: ..... to his father and his people: Behold... "What worship ye?"

They said, "We worship idols and we remain constantly in attendance on them."

Abraham said: "Do they listen to you when ye call (on them) or do you good or harm?"

They said: "Nay but we found our fathers doing thus, this is what we do."

Abraham said: "Do ye then see who ye have been worshipping Ye and your fathers before you?" "For they are enemies to me; not so the Lord and Cherisher of the Worlds Who created me and it is He Who guides me, Who gives me food and drink and when I am ill it is He Who cures me, Who will cause me to die and then to live (again) and Who I hope will forgive my faults on the Day of Judgment ..." "O my Lord!" "Bestow wisdom on me and join me with the righteous; Grant me honorable mention on the tongue of truth among the latest (generations) (Let my name live through many generations to come); make me one of the inheritors of the Garden of Bliss; forgive my father for that he is among those astray; and let me not be in disgrace on the Day when (men) will be raised up The Day whereon neither wealth nor sons will avail." "But only he (will prosper) that brings to Allah a sound heart."[9]

Abraham said to his father: "... O my father!" "Why worship that which heareth not and seeth not and can profit thee nothing?" "O my father!" "To me hath come knowledge which hath not reached thee: so follow me: I will guide thee to a Way that is even and straight. "O my father!" "Serve not Satan: for Satan is a rebel against (Allah) Most Gracious." "O my father!" "I fear lest a Penalty afflict thee from (Allah) Most Gracious so that thou become to Satan a friend."

The father replied: "Dost thou hate my gods O Abraham?" "If thou forbear not, I will indeed stone thee; now get away from me for a good long while!"

Abraham said: "Peace be on thee; I will pray to my Lord for thy forgiveness for He is to me Most Gracious, and I will turn away from you (all) and from those whom ye invoke besides Allah." "I will call on my Lord." Perhaps by my prayer to my Lord I shall be not unblessed."[10]

Abraham said to his father and his people: "What are these images to which ye are (so assiduously) devoted?"

They said: "We found our father worshipping them."

Abraham said: "Indeed ye have been in manifest error-ye and your fathers."

They said: "Have you brought us the Truth or are you one of those who jest?"

Abraham said: "Nay your Lord is the Lord of the heavens and the earth He Who created them (from nothing): and I am a witness to this (truth)." "And by Allah I have a plan for your idols after ye go away and turn your backs." ...So he broke them to pieces (all) but the biggest of them that they might turn (and address themselves) to it.

They said: "Who has done this to our gods?" "He must indeed be some man of impiety!"

Others among them said: "We heard a youth talk of them: he is called Abraham."

They said: "Then bring him before the eyes of the people that they may bear witness."

Those who went to fetch him said: "Art thou the one that did this with our gods O Abraham?"

Abraham said: "Nay this was done by their biggest one! Ask them if they can speak intelligently!"

So they spoke among themselves: "Surely ye are the ones in the wrong!" Then were they confounded with shame.

They said to Abraham: "Thou knowest full well that these (idols) do not speak!"

Abraham said: "Do ye then worship besides Allah things that can neither be of any good to you nor do you harm?" "Fie upon you and upon the things that ye worship besides Allah!" "Have ye no sense?"[11] "Is it false gods other than Allah that ye desire?" "Then what is your idea about the Lord of the Worlds?" Then did he cast a glance at the stars. And he said "I am indeed sick (at heart)!" So they turned away from him and departed.[12]

And Abraham prayed for his father's forgiveness only because of a promise he had made to him. But when it became clear to him that he was an enemy to Allah he dissociated himself from him for Abraham was most tenderhearted forbearing.[13]

In other words the Prophet Ibrahim left his Azar because he was an unbeliever.

Then did he turn to their gods and said, "Will ye not eat (of the offerings before you)?" "… What is the matter with you that ye speak not (intelligently)?" Then did he turn upon them striking (them) with the right hand. Then came (the worshippers) with hurried steps and faced (him). He said: "Worship ye that which ye have (yourselves) carved?" "But Allah has created you and your handwork!"[14] "… I do indeed clear myself of what ye worship: "(I worship) only Him Who made me and He will certainly guide me."

And he left it as a Word to endure among those who came after him that they may turn back (to Allah). Yea I have given the good things of this life to these (men) and their fathers until the Truth has come to them and an Apostle making things clear.[15]

The unbelievers said: "Build him a furnace and throw him into the blazing fire! … [16] "… Slay him or burn him…"

Abraham said: "For you ye have taken (for worship) idols besides Allah out of mutual love and regard between yourselves in this life; but on the Day of Judgment ye shall disown each other and curse each other: and your abode will be the Fire and ye shall have none to help.[17]

They said: "Burn him and protect your gods if ye do (anything at all)!"[18]

… But Allah did save him from the fire: verily in this are Signs for people who believe.[19] We said, O fire! Be thou cool and (a means of) safety for Abraham! Then, they sought a stratagem against him, but We made them the ones that lost most! We delivered him and (his nephew) Lut (and directed them) to the land which We have blessed for the nations and We bestowed on him Isaac and as an additional gift (a grandson) Jacob and We made righteous men of every one (of them). And We made them leaders guiding (men) by Our Command and We sent them inspiration to do good deeds to establish regular prayers and to practice regular charity; and they constantly served Us (and Us only).[20]

After the Prophet Ibrahim was saved from the fire, some joined him in faith while others saw him to be a threat and exiled him.

Before leaving Abraham said to his people: "…Serve Allah and fear Him: that will be best for you if ye understand!" "For ye do worship idols besides Allah and ye invent falsehood. The things that ye worship besides Allah have no power to give you sustenance. Then seek ye sustenance from Allah serve Him and be grateful to Him. To Him will be your return." "And if ye reject (the Message) so did generations before you and the duty of the apostle is only to preach publicly (and clearly)."[21]

But Lut had faith in Him.

Lut said: "I will leave home for the sake of my Lord for He is Exalted in Might and Wise."

And We gave (Abraham) Isaac and Jacob and ordained among his progeny Prophethood and Revelation and We granted him his reward in this life; and he was in the Hereafter (of the company) of the Righteous.[22] And We bestowed of Our Mercy on them and We granted them lofty honor on the tongue of truth.[23]

The Prophet Ibrahim spent his life reasoning against idol worshippers or people who proclaimed themselves as Gods. In fact, when King Nemrud, heard the Prophet Ibrahim had been mysteriously salvaged from the fire, he feared that he might challenge the status of his own god and summoned him to the palace. The dialogue that took place between them was cut short as a result of the Prophet Ibrahim's reasoning and intelligence.

Hast thou not turned thy vision to one who disputed with Abraham about his Lord because Allah had granted him power?

Abraham said: "My Lord is He Who Giveth life and death."

He said: "I give life and death."

Abraham said: "But it is Allah that causeth the sun to rise from the East do thou then cause him to rise from the West." Thus was he confounded who (in arrogance) rejected faith. Nor doth Allah give guidance to a people unjust.[24]

Even though there is no room for doubt in Islam, the Prophet Ibrahim wanted God to demonstrate how He was going to be able to resurrect the dead. God strengthened the Prophet Ibrahim's faith by commanding him to cut up four birds, mix their body parts, divide them into four portions, and place them on top of four different hills. Then, he was to call them back in God's name. The Prophet Ibrahim complied, and the birds flew back to him with enormous speed.

Behold! Abraham said: "My Lord!" "Show me how thou givest life to the dead."

Allah revealed: "Dost thou not then believe?"

Abraham said: "Yea, but to satisfy my own understanding."

Allah revealed: "Take four birds; tame them to turn to thee; put a portion of them on every hill and call to them; they will come to thee (flying) with speed. Then know that Allah is Exalted in Power

Wise."[25]

There is for you an excellent example (to follow) in Abraham and those with him when (Abraham and the believers) they said to their people: "We are clear of you and of whatever ye worship besides Allah: we have rejected you and there has arisen between us and you enmity and hatred forever unless ye believe in Allah and Him alone": But not when Abraham said to his father: "I will pray for forgiveness for thee though I have no power (to get) aught on thy behalf from Allah." (Abraham and the believers prayed): "Our Lord!" "In Thee do we trust and to Thee do we turn in repentance: to Thee is (our) final Goal. "Our Lord!" "Make us not a (test and) trial for the Unbelievers but forgive us our Lord!" "For Thou art the Exalted in Might the Wise." There was indeed in them an excellent example for you to follow for those whose hope is in Allah and in the Last Day. But if any turn away truly Allah is Free of all Wants Worthy of all Praise.[26]

Abraham said: "O my Lord!" "Grant me a righteous (son)!" So We gave him the good news of a boy ready to suffer and forbear.[27]

This verse is in reference to Isma'il, the Prophet's first son, who lived in Mecca referred to as *Bakka* in the Qur'an. The Prophet Ibrahim had married Sara, a woman who was faithful to him and to Islam. However, Sara could not have children and from fear of old age and the likelihood of never being able to conceive, she suggested that her husband conceive a child through her servant Hajar. Ultimately, Hajar gave birth to the Prophet Isma'il. Shortly after his birth, the Prophet Ibrahim was directed through a vision to take Hajar and Isma'il to the barren mountains of the Mecca. See chapter 8 on the Prophet Isma'il for more details.

Years later, the Prophet Ibrahim and his wife Sara, who had become menopausal and had lost any hope of having a child, were visited by two angels. They appeared as strangers to inform them that Sara was going to give birth to a son. In alarm, Sara found the news to be incredible and questioned the possibility. The angels informed her that what sounds impossible to humans could be made possible if God commands.

Allah's messengers came to Abraham and said: "Peace!"

Abraham said: "Peace!" and hastened to entertain them with a roasted calf." But when he saw their hands went not towards the (meal) he felt some mistrust of them and conceived a fear of them.[28]

They said: "Fear not!" "We give thee glad tidings of a son endowed with wisdom." He said: "Do ye give me glad tidings that old age has seized me"? "Of what then is your good news?"[29]

And his wife was standing (there) and she laughed: but We gave her glad tidings of Isaac and after him of Prophet Jacob.

Sara Abraham's wife said: "Alas for me!" "Shall I bear a child seeing I am an old woman and my husband here is an old man?" "That would indeed be a wonderful thing!"

They said: "Dost thou wonder at Allah's decree?" "The grace of Allah and His blessings on you O ye people of the house!" "For He is indeed worthy of all praise full of all glory!"[30] "We give thee glad tidings in truth: be not then in despair!"

Abraham said: "And who despairs of the mercy of his Lord but such as go astray?" "What then is the business on which ye (have come) O ye messengers (of Allah)?"[31]

They said: "We have been sent to a people (deep) in sin." "... Fear not: we have been sent against the people of Lut."[32] "... We have been sent to a people (deep) in sin to bring on them (a shower of) stones of clay (brimstone) marked as from thy Lord for those who trespass beyond bounds."[33]

The Prophet Lut, predestined by God, was a firm believer in Islam. However, the people of his community practiced homosexuality. As a result, God decided to do away with them completely.

When fear had passed from (the mind of) Abraham and the glad tidings had reached him he began to plead with Us for Lot's people. For Abraham was without doubt forbearing (of faults) compassionate and given to look to Allah.

Allah revealed: "O Abraham!" "Seek not this." "The decree of thy Lord hath gone forth: for them there cometh a Penalty that cannot be turned back!"[34] Then, We evacuated those of the Believers who were there. However, We found not there any just (Muslim) persons except in one house: And We left there a Sign for others to see and fear such Grievous Penalty.[35]

Abraham said: "O my Lord!" "Make this city one of peace and security: and preserve me and my sons from worshipping idols." "O my Lord!" "They have indeed led astray many among mankind: he then who follows my (ways) is of me and he who disobeys me (he acknowledges that their fate will be left to Allah's mercy), but thou art indeed Oft-Forgiving Most Merciful." "O our Lord!" "I have made some of my offspring to dwell in a valley without cultivation by thy Sacred House; in order O our Lord that they may establish regular prayer: so fill the hearts of some among men with love towards them and feed them with Fruits: so that they may give thanks."[36] "O our Lord!" "Truly Thou dost know what we conceal and what we reveal: for nothing whatever is hidden from Allah whether on earth or in heaven." "Praise be to Allah who hath granted unto me in old age Isma'il and Isaac: for truly my Lord is He the Hearer of Prayer!" "O my Lord!" "Make me one who establishes regular Prayer and also (raise such) among my offspring O our Lord! And accept Thou my Prayer." "O our Lord!" "Cover (us) with Thy Forgiveness me my parents and (all)

Believers on the Day that the Reckoning will be established!"[37]

Some considerable time after the separation between the Prophet Ibrahim and his son Isma'il, Prophet Ibrahim went to Mecca to visit with him. God connected with the Prophet Ibrahim through a vision putting him once more to the test. As difficult as this might have been for the Prophet Ibrahim, he revealed to his son that he had a vision to offer him in sacrifice. Submitting their wills to God, the Prophet Ibrahim took his son near mount *Mina* in Mecca, Saudi Arabia, and laid him prostrate on his forehead until God intervened. Satisfied with the Prophet Ibrahim's willingness to comply, He ransomed Isma'il with a sheep. In commemoration of this very event sheep are sacrificed during the *Hajj* or pilgrimage period by Muslims all over the world. Today, Prophet Isma'il is known as the Patriarch of the Arab race.

Then when (the son) reached (the age of) (serious) work with him...

(Abraham) said: "O my son! I see in vision that I offer thee in sacrifice: now see what is thy view!"

The son said: "O my father!" "Do as thou art commanded: thou will find me if Allah so wills one practicing Patience and Constancy!"

So when they had both submitted their wills (to Allah) and He had laid Him prostrate on his forehead (for sacrifice)

We (Allah) called out to him: "O Abraham!" "Thou hast already fulfilled the vision!"

Thus indeed do We reward those who do right. For this was obviously a trial and We ransomed him with a momentous sacrifice: And We left (this blessing—the sacrifice of sheep) for him among generations (to come) in later times: "Peace and salutation to Abraham!" Thus indeed do We reward those who do right. For he was one of Our believing Servants. And We gave him the good news of Isaac a prophet one of the Righteous. We blessed him and Isaac: but of their progeny are (some) that do right and (some) that obviously do wrong to their own souls.[38]

Ye people of the Book! Why dispute ye about Abraham when the Law and the Gospel were not revealed till after him? Have ye no understanding? Ah! Ye are those who fell to disputing (even) in matters of which ye had some knowledge! But why dispute ye in matters of which ye have no knowledge? It is Allah Who knows and ye who know not! Abraham was not a Jew nor yet a Christian, but he was true in faith and bowed his will to Allah's (which is Islam) and he joined not gods with Allah. Without doubt among men the nearest of kin to Prophet Abraham are those who follow him as are also this Apostle and those who believe; and Allah is the Protector of those who have faith.[39]

Here, God is informing Prophet Muhammad *(pbuh)* of the truth regarding the Prophet Ibrahim and is directing him to relate this information to the unbelievers:

Say: "Allah speaketh the truth: follow the religion of Prophet Abraham the sane in faith; he was not of the pagans."[40]

It is those who believe and confuse not their beliefs with wrong that are (truly) in security for they are on (right) guidance. That was the reasoning about Us which We gave to Abraham (to use) against his people: We raise whom We will degree after degree: for thy Lord is full of wisdom and knowledge. We gave him Isaac and Jacob: all (three) We guided: and before him We guided Noah and among his progeny David, Solomon, Job, Joseph, Moses, and Aaron: thus do We reward those who do good.[41]

Abraham was indeed a model devoutly obedient to Allah (and) true in faith and he joined not gods with Allah: He showed his gratitude for the favors of Allah Who chose him and guided him to a straight way. And We gave him good in this world and he will be in the Hereafter in the ranks of the righteous. Therefore, We have taught thee the inspired (message) Follow the ways of Abraham the true in faith and he joined not gods with Allah.

According to Qur'anic exegesis, Sabbath was instituted with the Law of the Prophet Musa. God states that there were disputes among those who believed in the Old Testament and those who believed in the New One as to whether Saturday or Sunday should be the designated day for prayer and worship. Because of these disputes, He will settle their differences on the Day of Judgment.

> The Sabbath was made strictly for those who disagreed (as to its observance); but Allah will judge between them on the Day of Judgment as to their differences.[42]

During the time of the Prophet Ibrahim, there were no designated places for Muslims to worship God. As the believers in Islam began to increase, God ordered the Prophet Ibrahim to build a Sacred House, the *Kabaa*. The *Kabaa* (*Al Masjid Al-Haram*) located in Mecca is the center of the holy place of worship in Islam. The word *Kabaa* means cube in Arabic. It is a cube-shaped stone structure built in the middle of the Sacred Mosque. It is a landmark for the House of God. The Prophet Ibrahim was ordered to build it on a hill higher than the land surrounding it. Isma'il brought the stones, and the Prophet Ibrahim built the walls. Once it was completed, Archangel Jibril descended from heaven and showed the Prophet Ibrahim the *Hajj* rituals of the time. Today, this is where pilgrims from all over the Muslim world perform the *Hajj* and visit the *Kabaa* at a specified time each year or to perform *Umrah* and visit the *Kabaa* any time of the year outside of the *Hajj* period to perform *Hajj*-like rituals.

> The first House (of worship) appointed for men was that at Bakka (Mecca) full of blessing and of guidance for all kinds of beings. In it are signs manifest; (for example) the Station of Abraham; whoever enters it attains security; pilgrimage thereto is a duty men owe to Allah those who can afford the journey; but if any deny faith Allah stands not in need of any of his creatures.[43]

Remember We made the house a place of assembly for men and a place of safety; and take ye the station of Abraham as a place of prayer; and We covenanted with Abraham and Isma'il that they should sanctify My House for those who compass it round or use it as a retreat or bow or prostrate themselves (therein in prayer). And remember Abraham said: "My Lord make this a City of Peace and feed its people with fruits such of them as believe in Allah and the Last Day." He revealed: "(Yea) and such as reject faith for a while will I grant them their pleasure but will soon drive them to the torment of fire an evil destination (indeed)!" And remember Abraham and Isma'il raised the foundations of the House (with this prayer): "Our Lord!" "Accept (this service) from us for thou art the All-Hearing the All-Knowing." "Our Lord!" "Make of us Muslims bowing to Thy (Will) and of our progeny a people Muslim bowing to Thy (Will) and show us our places for the celebration of (due) rites; and turn unto us (in mercy); for Thou art the Oft-Returning Most-Merciful. And who turns away from the religion of Abraham but such as debase their souls with folly?" Him We chose and rendered pure in this world: and he will be in the Hereafter in the ranks of the righteous.[44]

Behold! We gave the site to Abraham of the (Sacred) House (saying): Associate not any thing (in worship) with Me; and sanctify My House for those who compass it round or stand up or bow or prostrate themselves (therein in prayer).[45] And strive in His cause as ye ought to strive (with sincerity and under discipline): He has chosen you and has imposed no difficulties on you in religion; it is the cult of your father Abraham. It is He Who has named you Muslims both before and in this (Revelation); that the Apostle may be a witness for you and ye be witnesses for mankind! So establish regular Prayer give regular Charity and hold fast to Allah! He is your Protector the Best to protect and the Best to help![46]

And commemorate Our servants Abraham Isaac and Jacob possessors of Power and Vision. Verily We did chose them for a special (purpose) proclaiming the Message of the Hereafter. They were in Our sight truly of the company of the Elect and the Good. And commemorate Isma'il, Elisha, and Dhul-Kifl: each of them was of the company of the Good.[47]

And this was the legacy that Abraham left to his sons and so did Jacob; "O my sons!" Allah hath chosen the faith for you; then die not except in the faith of Islam." "Were ye witnesses when death appeared before Jacob?" Behold he said to his sons: "What will ye worship after me?" They said: "We shall worship thy Allah and the Allah of thy fathers of Abraham, Isma'il, and Isaac the one (true) Allah to Him we bow (in Islam)."[48]

The Prophet Ibrahim lived to worship God and spread the teachings of Islam through his children and their offspring. He yearned for a world free of conflict and knew that man was created to pursue one unified world of creation while setting aside any doubt of God's existence. He dedicated his entire life to promote peace within himself and within his nation. He understood that to believe in God was to believe in sacrificing from one's own cravings or desires for worldly matters even if it meant the sacrifice of a child. He wanted his people to trust in God's magnificence so that they too could ultimately be led to eternal peace.

Chapter 7

Prophet Lut—*Lot*

The Prophet Lut, the Prophet Ibrahim's nephew, lived in the city of Sodom located on the western shore of the Dead Sea. The people of his town were lazy, evil, and immoral thieves. They also acted against God's commands and practiced homosexuality. God inspired the Prophet Lut to inform them that if they did not stop such ill practices, He would spread His calamity among them. They refused to believe and tried to drive the Prophet Lut out of the city.

Eventually, God sent two men (His angels) to visit the Prophet Lut; they explained to him that they wanted to be his guest for a few days. The Prophet Lut agreed, but his wife immediately informed the townspeople, and they rushed to his home. They tried to sexually assault the men, but became angry and left when they realized that the two men were angels. Shortly thereafter, the angels warned the Prophet Lut to depart from the city at sunrise, but to leave his wife behind who essentially was an unbeliever. The Prophet Lut complied, and the city Sodom was shaken by an earthquake and destroyed by a storm made of stones.[1] The Prophet Lut knew that those who practiced homosexuality were doing so against God's will, which the union of a man and a woman was ordained by God, and thus that it was wrong to trespass the sphere of this mandate. He followed the footsteps of his uncle, the Prophet Ibrahim, and yearned for a world of peace within himself and the believers.

> When Our Messengers came to Abraham with the good news they said: "We are indeed going to destroy the people of this township: for truly they are (addicted to) crime."

> Abraham said: "…But there is Lut there."

> Allah's messengers said: "…Well do." "We know who is there and we will certainly save him and his followers except his wife: she is of those who lag behind!"[2]

God's fine-looking young messengers (angels) visited the Prophet Lut after he had tried endlessly to advise his people against homosexuality. They explained to the Prophet Lut that God's plan was to demolish both Sodom and its companion city Gomorrah, and all those who condoned the practice of homosexuality. God has made it clear throughout various verses in the Qur'an that He created women to become men's sexual companions, not men. Therefore, deviating from this is a sin.

> Lut said to his people: "… Will ye not fear Allah?" "I am to you an apostle worthy of all trust." "So fear Allah and obey me."[3] "Do ye indeed approach men and cut off the highway and practice wickedness (even) in your councils?" But his people gave no answer but this:

> They said: "Bring us the Wrath of Allah if thou tellest the truth."[4]

> Lut said: "No reward do I ask of you for it: my reward is only from the Lord of the Worlds." "Of all the creatures in the world will ye approach males and leave those whom Allah has created for you to be your mates?" "Nay ye are a people transgressing (all limits)!"

They said: "If thou desist not O Lut!" "Thou wilt assuredly be cast out!"

Lut said: "I do detest your doings." "O my Lord!" "Deliver me and my family from such things as they do!"[5] "... This is a distressful day."[6] "Ye appear to be uncommon folk."

They said: "Yea we have come to thee to accomplish that of which they doubt." "We have brought to thee that which is inevitably due and assuredly we tell the truth."[7]

Lut said: "These are my guests: disgrace me not: But fear Allah and shame me not."

They said: "Did we not forbid thee (to speak) for all and sundry?"[8]

At the time of their arrival, the Prophet Lut and the inhabitants of his city had no idea who the young men were, but God was ready to put an end to perversity. He constantly reminds us not to dispute his warnings and to believe in the Day of Judgment. He is gracious to those who believe and show appreciation, but will punish those who reject His warnings.

Lut said: "...O my people!" "Here are my daughters: they are purer for you (if ye marry)!" Lut was attempting to offer his daughters in marriage. "Now fear Allah and cover me not with shame about my guests!" "Is there not among you a single right-minded man?"

They said: "Well dost thou know we have no need of thy daughters: indeed thou knowest quite well what we want!"

By offering women to the transgressors, Prophet Lut was referring to city girls and not necessarily his own daughters when he said that it was wiser and better for them to have a relationship with women, not men.

Lut said: "Would that I had power to suppress you or that I could betake myself to some powerful support."[9] Excepting the adherents of Lut: them, we are certainly (charged) to save (from harm) except his wife who we have ascertained will be among those who will lag behind."[10]

Then, once with Lut, (The Messengers) said: "O Lut!" "We are Messengers from thy Lord!" "By no means shall they reach thee!" "Now travel with thy family while yet a part of the night remains and let not any of you look back: but thy wife (will remain behind): to her will happen what happens to the people." "Morning is their time appointed: is not the morning nigh?" When Our decree issued We turned (the cities) upside down and rained down on them brimstones hard as baked clay spread layer on layer. Marked as from thy Lord: nor are they ever far from those who do wrong![11]

Behold! In this are Signs for those who by tokens do understand. And the (cities were) right on the highroad. Behold! In this is a Sign for those who believe![12]

Allah addresses unbelievers: "Would ye really approach men in your lusts rather than women?" "Nay ye are a people (grossly) ignorant!" However, his people gave no other answer but this:

They said: "Drive out the followers of Lut from your city: these are indeed men who want to be clean and pure."[13]

In the end, a world of peace should rise above all worldly troubles at the individual and family levels. The Prophet Lut and his followers lived through the reign and terror of homosexuals who raped other men and young boys who refused to consent to their sexual advances. He feared that the family unit was subject to breaking up from the ways of those who preferred to act on their unnatural desires, but God, All Knowing, responded to his fear by liberating him and his followers from the wrath of his people.

Chapter 8

Prophet Isma'il—*Ishmael*

According to the Qur'an, Isma'il was the Prophet Ibrahim's firstborn son. When his wife Sara realized that she was barren and that her husband had yearned for a son, she suggested that he conceive a child through Hajar, who, according to Qur'anic exegesis, was Sara's servant. Eventually, Hajar became pregnant with Isma'il.

> Abraham said: "My lord!" "Grant me a righteous (son)!" So we gave him the good news of a boy possessing forbearance."[1]

Once he was born, Sara began to dislike Hajar and complained frequently to her husband. The Prophet Ibrahim called out to his Lord for assistance and when Isma'il was not even a year old, the Prophet Ibrahim was instructed by God through a vision to take Hajar and his son to Mecca (*Bakka*) and to leave them there. Mecca was not inhabited at the time, and the Prophet Ibrahim was worried, but he trusted that God would watch over them.

> "O our Lord! I have made some of my offspring to dwell in a valley without cultivation, by Thy Sacred House; in order, O our Lord, that they may establish regular Prayer: so fill the hearts of some among men with love towards them, and feed them with

fruits: so that they may give thanks."[2]

Hajar was apprehensive and questioned the Prophet Ibrahim. He informed her that he was following God's command, and once she surrendered to her fate, she began to search for water. She thought that she had seen signs of water near the hill of *Marwa* and began to run. While dashing toward nothing more than a delusion, she lost sight of her son and ran back and forth between the two hills of *Safa* and *Marwa* seven times until she found him. This running back and forth seven times is carried out by pilgrims during the *Hajj* period in Mecca each year. The ground had miraculously broken open, and Hajar found her son tapping at a spring of water beneath his feet. In trying to preserve the water, she began to gather sand around it. The act of gathering sand around water or drawing it together means *zama* in Arabic. This verb gave the water its current name, *Zamzam* water, water that continues to quench the thirst of millions of Muslims during pilgrimage today. Others believe that the word *zamzam* is not an Arabic word and that it comes from the ancient Egyptian language. If this is true, then the word *zamzam* means "stop."

As a result, birds and wild beasts flocked toward the water, and a clan of men approached Hajar asking her who she was and what relation she had with the child. She responded by informing them that she was the mother of Isma'il, the son of the Prophet Ibrahim. She told them that the Prophet Ibrahim was instructed by God through a vision to leave her and her son in the barren valley of Mecca. They asked her for permission to camp around her site to benefit from the water. She told them that she would have to get permission from the Prophet Ibrahim first. The Prophet Ibrahim visited her on the third day, and she informed him of the clan's request. He endorsed the request, giving the clan the right to remain near the spring, provided that they offer protection to Hajar and her son, Isma'il. They gratefully pitched their tents, and when the Prophet Ibrahim returned anew, he was amazed at the number of people who were living around Hajar and his son. He returned to his home knowing that God is indeed merciful and compassionate.[3]

When Isma'il grew older, God instructed the Prophet Ibrahim through a vision to rebuild the *Kabaa* that had been built by the

Prophet Adam and later displaced by a flood. He did so willingly, but with great difficulty.

The Prophet Ibrahim had a vision that he was slaughtering his son Isma'il.

Then when (the son) reached (the age of) (serious) work with him ...

(Abraham) said: "O my son! I see in vision that I offer thee in sacrifice: now see what is thy view!"

The son said: "O my father!" "Do as thou art commanded: thou wilt find me if Allah so wills one practicing Patience and Constancy!"

So when they had both submitted their wills (to Allah) and He had laid Him prostrate on his forehead (for sacrifice) ...

We (Allah) called out to him: "O Abraham!" "Thou hast already fulfilled the vision!"

The Prophet Ibrahim shared his vision with his son to see if he was ready to accept God's command. His son expressed readiness by informing his father that he is willing to comply with God's request. While preparing for the sacrifice, the Archangel Jibril stopped the Prophet Ibrahim, instructing him to sacrifice a sheep instead. The dream appeared to be more symbolic of a test of faith than it was for the Prophet Ibrahim to literally sacrifice his only son. God does not approve of human sacrifice anywhere in the Qur'an, yet the Prophet Ibrahim's compliance and willingness to sacrifice his son in the name of God is celebrated in *Eid ul-Adha* (end of *Hajj* holiday) every year by Muslims.

Thus indeed do We reward those who do right. For this was obviously a trial and We ransomed him with a momentous sacrifice: And We left (this blessing—the sacrifice of sheep) for him among generations (to come) in later times: "Peace and salutation to Abraham!" Thus indeed do We reward those who do right. For he was one of Our believing Servants. And We gave him the good news of Isaac a prophet one of the Righteous. We blessed him and Isaac: but of their progeny are (some) that do right and (some) that obviously do wrong to their own souls.[4]

"...Our Lord: Accept from us, surely you are the hearing, the knowing. Our Lord! Make us both submissive to you and raise from our offspring a nation submitting to you and show us ways of devotion and turn to us mercifully. You are the Oft-returning to mercy, the most merciful."[5]

The Prophet Muhammad *(pbuh)* is a direct descendant of the Prophet Isma'il, thus confirming that the Prophet Ibrahim was a Muslim (one who submits him/herself to God) in that he, too, submitted his will to God and believed in His oneness. This contradicts the Jewish notion that the Prophet Ibrahim was a Jew, and thus, according to the Qur'an Jews, Christians, and Muslims share the same ancestral heritage and are considered descendants of the Prophet Ibrahim.

Ye people of the Book! Why dispute ye about Abraham when the Law and the Gospel were not revealed till after him? Have ye no understanding? Ah! Ye are those who fell to disputing (even) in matters of which ye had some knowledge! But why dispute ye in matters of which ye have no knowledge? It is Allah Who knows and ye who know not! Abraham was not a Jew nor yet a Christian, but he was true in faith and bowed his will to Allah's (which is Islam) and he joined not gods with Allah. Without doubt among men the nearest of kin to Prophet Abraham are those who follow him as are also this Apostle and those who believe; and Allah is the Protector of those who have faith.[6]

The Prophet Isma'il established a true family, a true clan, and a true tribe in the heart of Mecca, the primary residence of the Prophet Adam. He became the nucleus of peace embracing all of God's creation. He followed the footsteps of his father and was the center of harmony among his people, devoting his mind, heart, and soul to God. Historians claim that at the time of his death, Isma'il was buried near the *Kabaa* in Mecca.

Chapter 9

Prophet Ishaq—*Isaac*

Ishaq was the Prophet Ibrahim's second son, who was born when the Prophet Ibrahim was approximately 110 years old, and his wife Sara was menopausal and graying.

> "They said: "Fear not!" "We give thee glad tidings of a son endowed with wisdom." He said: "Do ye give me glad tidings that old age has seized me"? "Of what then is your good news?"[1]

> And his wife was standing (there) and she laughed: but We gave her glad tidings of Isaac and after him of Yaqub.

> Sara Abraham's wife said: "Alas for me!" "Shall I bear a child seeing I am an old woman and my husband here is an old man?" "That would indeed be a wonderful thing!"

> They said: "Dost thou wonder at Allah's decree?" "The grace of Allah and His blessings on you O ye people of the house!" "For He is indeed worthy of all praise full of all glory!"[2] "We give thee

glad tidings in truth: be not then in despair!"[3]

Sara was in shock to learn that she was going to become pregnant at her age, but she made a miraculous mark in history and gave birth to the Prophet Ishaq. The Prophet Ishaq lived a joyful life under the prophethood of his father the Prophet Ibrahim, and he later married and gave birth to the Prophet Yaqub.[4] The Prophet Ishaq instructed his son, the Prophet Yaqub, to assume his mission, as he had assumed his own father's, and guide people to pray and worship God so that he might leave this world satisfied. Even though the Prophet Ishaq bears little mention in the Qur'an, he was the longest living patriarch, ancestor of the Prophet Musa, and the father of Judaism.[5] He embodied peace and gave birth to a nation of peaceful and monotheistic believers.

Chapter 10

Prophet Yaqub—*Jacob*

The Prophet Yaqub, the son of the Prophet Ishaq, was favored by his father, and God gifted him with prophethood. According to the Qur'an, God endowed him with wisdom, and he was given knowledge beyond the ordinary person. He married two women and had many children.

The Prophet Yaqub was very fond of his son Yusuf. When he realized that his love for Yusuf created sibling jealousy and rivalry, he worried about Yusuf when he was with them. Unfortunately, vainly hoping that the Prophet Yaqub would transfer his love from Yusuf to them, the cruel brothers threw Yusuf into a dry well. They lied to their father and told him that he had been eaten by a wolf while they were engaged in other activities. The Prophet Yaqub did not believe his sons and trusted that God would ease his pain and watch over Yusuf, since he believed that Yusuf had been chosen by God to be a Prophet. He thought that if he was patient enough, God would grant that he might see his son again. His belief in God and conviction that He is kind, loving, and merciful led him to direct his children and his people to join him in his belief in the religion of Prophet Ibrahim and not spend their lives in greed and self-indulgence.

And who turns away from the religion of Abraham but such as debase their souls with folly? Him We chose and rendered pure in this world: and he will be in the Hereafter in the ranks of the righteous. Behold! His Lord revealed to him: Bow (thy will to me). He said: "I bow (my will) to the Lord and Cherisher of the universe."

And this was the legacy that Abraham left to his sons and so did Yaqub; "O my sons!" "Allah hath chosen the faith for you; then die not except in the faith of Islam." Were ye witnesses when death appeared before Yaqub? Behold he said to his sons: "What will ye worship after me?" They said: "We shall worship thy Allah and the Allah of thy fathers of Abraham Isma'il and Isaac the one (true) Allah to Him we bow (in Islam)." That was a People that hath passed away. They shall reap the fruit of what they did and ye of what ye do! Of their merits there is no question in your case! They say: "Become Jews or Christians if ye would be guided (to salvation)." Say thou: "Nay!" "(I would rather) the religion of Abraham the true and he joined not gods with Allah." Say ye: We believe in Allah and the revelation given to us and to Abraham, Isma'il, Isaac, Yaqub, and the Tribes and given to Musa and Jesus and to (all) Prophets from their Lord we make no difference between one and another of them and we bow to Allah (in Islam).

So if they believe as ye believe they are indeed on the right path; but if they turn back it is they who are in schism; but Allah will suffice thee as against them and He is the All-Hearing the All-Knowing. (Our religion is) the baptism of Allah; and who can baptize better than Allah? And it is He whom we worship. Say: Will ye dispute with us about Allah seeing that He is our Lord and your Lord; that we are responsible for our doings and ye for yours; and that we are sincere (in our faith) in Him? Or do ye say that Abraham, Isma'il, Isaac, Yaqub, and the Tribes were Jews or Christians? Say: Do ye know better than Allah? Ah! Who is more unjust than those who conceal the testimony they have from Allah? But Allah is not unmindful of what ye do![1]

But verily thy Lord to those who do wrong in ignorance - but who thereafter repent and make amends thy Lord - after all this, is Oft-Forgiving Most Merciful. Abraham was indeed a model, devoutly obedient to Allah, (and) true in Faith, and he joined not gods with Allah. He showed his gratitude for the favors of Allah Who chose him and guided him to a straight way. And We gave him good in this world, and he will be in the Hereafter, in the ranks of the righteous. So We have taught thee the inspired (message), "Follow the ways of Abraham the true in faith and he joined not gods with Allah."[2]

The Prophet Yaqub stood in history as an honorable Prophet and entered a high position with God. He knew that it was essential to spread his belief in the One God and united his people in a peaceful way. He managed to start his own family by making peace the center of his life and viably his primary objective.

Chapter 11

Prophet Yusuf—*Joseph*

The story of the Prophet Yusuf, born around 906 BCE in Canaan, Palestine, is a miracle from God that exposes the reader to another of God's plans meant to educate man on the importance of peace and tolerance. The Prophet Yusuf was the son of the Prophet Yaqub, and the great grandson of the Prophet Ibrahim. The Prophet Yaqub had twelve sons from two different wives, and the Prophet Yusuf and his brother Benjamin were the sons of Rachel. The Prophet Yaqub was about ninety years old when the Prophet Yusuf was born. At about the age of six, his father established residence in the town of Hebron.[1]

The story of the Prophet Yusuf was revealed to Prophet Muhammad *(pbuh)* at a time when the *Quraish*, the Prophet's *(pbuh)* own kinsmen, were considering his persecution, exile, or imprisonment. They tested his prophethood by asking him, "Why did the Israelites go to Egypt?" This question was asked because they knew that their story was not known to the Arabs, for there was no mention of it whatever in their traditions, and the Holy Prophet *(pbuh)* had never even referred to it before. Therefore, they were sure that he would fail in his response. But, contrary to their expectations, the Prophet Muhammad *(pbuh)* recited the story of the Prophet Yusuf. This put the *Quraish* in a very awkward position because it not only foiled their scheme but also shed light on what might happen to them if they were to continue to follow the path of the unbelievers. This was perhaps their warning to refrain from sin, treachery and idolatry.[2]

Behold Joseph said to his father: "O my father, I did see eleven stars and the sun and the moon: I saw them prostrate themselves to me!"

His father said: "My (dear) little son, relate not thy vision to thy brothers lest they concoct a plot against thee: for Satan is to man an avowed enemy!" "Thus will thy Lord choose thee and teach thee the interpretation of stories (and events) and perfect His favor to thee and to the posterity of Prophet Jacob even as He perfected it to thy fathers Prophet Abraham and Isaac aforetime!" "For Allah is full of knowledge and wisdom."

The Prophet Yusuf's brothers were indeed very jealous of him and were determined to permanently dispose of him.

Verily in Joseph and his brethren are Signs (or Symbols) for Seekers (after Truth).

They said: "Truly Joseph and his brother are loved more by our father than we: but we are a goodly body!" "Really our father is obviously wandering (in his mind)!" "Slay ye Joseph or cast him out to some (unknown) land that so the favor of your father may be given to you alone: (There will be time enough) for you to be righteous after that!"

One of them said: "Slay not Joseph but if ye must do something throw him down to the bottom of the well: he will be picked up by some caravan of travelers."

They began their plot and... said: "O our father, why dost thou not trust us with Joseph seeing we are indeed his sincere well-wishers?" "Send him with us tomorrow to enjoy himself and play and we shall take every care of him."

Jacob said: "Really it saddens me that ye should take him away: I fear lest the wolf should devour him while ye attend not to him."

They said: "If the wolf were to devour him while we are (so large) a party then should we indeed (first) have perished ourselves!" So they did take him away and they all agreed to throw him down to the bottom of the well: and We put into his heart (this Message): Of a surety thou shalt (one day) tell them the truth of this their affair while they know (thee) not. Then they came to their father in the early part of the night weeping. "Oh our father, we went racing with one another and left Joseph with our things: and the wolf devoured him." "But thou wilt never believe us even though we tell the truth." They stained his shirt with false blood.

Jacob said: "Nay but your minds have made up a tale (that may pass) with you." "For me, patience is most fitting: against that which ye assert it is Allah (alone) whose help can be sought."

Then there came a caravan of travelers: they sent their water-carrier (for water) and he let down his bucket (into the well)...

The Travelers said: "Ah there!" "Good news!" "Here is a (fine) young man!" "So they concealed him as a treasure!" But, Allah knoweth well all that they do! The (travelers) sold him for a miserable price for a few dirhams counted out: in such low estimation did they hold him!

The King of the Hyksos Dynasty in Egypt bought him between the nineteenth and seventeenth century BCE. The King said to his wife:

"Make his stay (among us) honorable: maybe he will bring us much good or we shall adopt him as a son."

Thus did we establish Joseph in the land that We might teach him the interpretation of stories (and events). And Allah hath full power and control over His affairs; but most among mankind know it not. When Joseph attained his full manhood, We gave him power and knowledge: thus do We reward those who do right.

But she (Zulaikha) in whose house he was sought to seduce him from his (true) self.

She fastened the doors and said: "Now come thou (dear one)!"

He (Joseph) said: "Allah forbid!" "Truly (thy husband) is my lord!" "He made my sojourn agreeable!" "Truly to no good come those who do wrong!" And (with passion) did she desire him and he would have desired her but that he saw the evidence of his Lord: thus (did We order) that We might turn away from him (all) evil and shameful deeds: for he was one of Our servants sincere and purified. So they both raced each other to the door and she tore his shirt from the back: they both found her lord near the door.

She said: "What is the (fitting) punishment for one who formed an evil design against thy wife but prison or a grievous chastisement?"

When the Prophet Yusuf realized that her husband who saw them both was standing at the door …

He said: "It was she that sought to seduce me from my (true) self." And one of her household saw (this) and bore witness (thus): "If it be that his shirt is torn from the front then is her tale true and he is a liar!" "But if it be that his shirt is torn from the back then is she the liar and he is telling the truth!"

So when he saw his shirt that it was torn at the back…

Her husband said: "Behold!" "It is a snare of you women!" "Truly mighty is your snare!" "O Joseph pass this over, (O wife) ask forgiveness for thy sin for truly thou hast been at fault!"

The word was out and Ladies in the City said: "The wife of the (great) Aziz is seeking to seduce her slave from his (true) self: truly hath he inspired her with violent love: we see she is evidently going astray."

When Zulaikha heard of their malicious talk she sent for them and prepared a banquet for them: she gave each of them a knife; and she said (to Prophet Joseph), "Come out before them." When they saw him they did extol him and (in their amazement) cut their hands…

They said: "Allah preserve us!" "No mortal is this!" "This is none other than a noble angel!"

She said: "There before you is the man about whom ye did blame me!" "I did seek to seduce him from his (true) self but he did firmly save himself guiltless!" "And now if he doth not my bidding he shall certainly be cast into prison and (what is more) be in the company of the vilest!"

Here, and with the support of other women of her status, Zulaikha was no longer ashamed of admitting that she wanted him to satisfy her own desires. In fact, she threatened him with prison if he refused to comply with her wishes.

He (Joseph) said: "O my Lord!" "The prison is more to my liking than that to which they invite me: unless thou turn away their snare from me I should (in my youthful folly) feel inclined towards them and join the ranks of the ignorant."

Therefore, his Lord heard him (in his prayer) and turned away from him their snare: verily He heareth and knoweth (all things). Then it occurred to the men after they had seen the Signs (that it was best) to imprison him for a time. Now with him there came into the prison two young men.

One of them said: "I see myself (in a dream) pressing wine."

The other said: "I see myself (in a dream) carrying bread on my head and birds are eating thereof." "Tell us (they said to Prophet Joseph) the truth and meaning thereof: for we see thou art one that doth well (to all)."

Joseph said: "Before any food comes (in due course) to feed either of you I will surely reveal to you the truth and meaning of this ere it come to pass: that is part of the (Duty) which my Lord hath taught me." "I have (I assure you) abandoned the ways of a people that believe not in Allah and that (even) deny the Hereafter." "And I follow the ways of my fathers Abraham, Isaac and Jacob; and never could we attribute any partners whatever to Allah: that (comes) of the grace of Allah to us and to mankind: yet most men are not grateful." "O my two companions of the prison!" "I ask you: are many lords differing among themselves better or Allah the One Supreme and Irresistible?" "If not Him ye worship nothing but names which ye have named, ye and your fathers for which Allah hath sent you no authority: the Command is for none but Allah: He hath commanded that ye worship none but Him: that is the right religion but Most men understand not ..." "O my two companions of the prison!" "As to one of you he will pour out the wine for his lord to drink: as for the other he will hang from the cross and the birds will eat from off his head. (So) hath been decreed that matter whereof ye twain do enquire ..." And of the two to that one whom he considered about to be saved he said: "Mention me to thy lord." But Satan made him forget to mention him to his lord: and (Prophet Joseph) lingered in prison a few (more) years.

The Prophet Yusuf interpreted their dreams. He informed them that he worshiped God and that he strongly advised them to do the same.

The king (of Egypt) said: "I do see (in a vision) seven fat kine (plural of cow) whom seven lean ones devour and seven green ears of corn and seven (others) withered." "O ye chiefs, expound to me my vision if it be that ye can interpret visions."

They said: "A confused medley of dreams: and we are not skilled in the interpretation of dreams."

But the man who had been released one of the two (who had been in prison) and who now bethought him after (so long) a space of time said: "I will tell you the truth of its interpretation: send ye me (therefore)."

The prisoner, who had been detained with the Prophet Yusuf and released, returned to see the Prophet Yusuf so that he might ask him to interpret the king's dream.

"O Joseph!" said the man: "O man of truth, expound to us (the dream) of seven fat kine whom seven lean ones devour and of seven green ears of corn and (seven) others withered: that I may return to the people and that they may understand."

Joseph said: "For seven years shall ye diligently sow as is your wont: and the harvests that ye reap ye shall leave them in the ear except a little of which ye shall eat." "Then will come after that (period) seven dreadful (years) which will devour what ye shall have laid aside in advance everyone except for a little which ye shall have (specially) guarded." "Then will come after that (period) a year in which the people will have abundant water and in which they will press (wine and oil)."

The ex-prisoner returned to the king and explained the dream according to the Prophet Yusuf's interpretation:

So the king said: "Bring ye him unto me." But when the messenger came to him ...

Joseph said: "Go thou back to thy lord and ask him -What is the state of mind of the ladies who cut their hands for my Lord is certainly well aware of their snare?"

The king said (to the ladies): "What was your affair when ye did seek to seduce Joseph from his (true) self?"

The ladies said: "Allah preserve us!" "No evil know we against him!"

The Aziz's wife said: "Now is the truth manifest (to all): it was I who sought to seduce him from his (true) self: he is indeed of those who are (ever) true (and virtuous)." "This (say I) in order that he may know that I have never been false to him in his absence and that Allah will never guide the snare of the false ones." "Nor do I absolve my own self (of blame): the (human soul) is certainly prone to evil unless my Lord bestows His Mercy, but surely certainly my Lord is Oft-Forgiving Most Merciful."

She confessed the truth to her husband and asked for his mercy.

So the king said: "Bring him unto me; I will take him specially to serve about my own person." Therefore, when he had spoken to him he said: "Be assured this day thou art before our own Presence with rank firmly established and fidelity fully proved!"

Joseph said: "Set me over the storehouses of the land: I will indeed guard them as one that knows (their importance)."

Thus did We give established power to Joseph in the land to take possession therein as when or where he pleased. We bestow of Our mercy on whom We please and We suffer not to be lost the reward of those who do good. But verily the reward of the Hereafter is the best for those who believe and are constant in righteousness.

As years passed and prosperity began to fade, famine took over the land, but the Prophet Yusuf had reserved enough food to meet the calamities. Not only did the Egyptians bless him, but neighboring countries began to purchase corn from Egypt. All purchasers were received with hospitality and were sold corn with judicious measure. However, the Prophet Yusuf's heart was unsettled as he thought of his poor father, the Prophet Yaqub, and his younger brother, Benjamin. The Prophet Yusuf also wondered whether his ten stepbrothers were going to be as cruel to Benjamin as they were with him.

Then came Joseph's brethren: they entered his presence and he (Prophet Joseph) knew them but they knew him not. And when he had furnished them forth with provisions (suitable) for them …

He (Joseph) said: "Bring unto me a brother ye have of the same father as yourselves (but a different mother): see ye not that I pay out full measure and that I do provide the best hospitality?" "Now if ye bring him not to me ye shall have no measure (of corn) from me nor shall be ye (even) come near me."

They said: "We shall certainly seek to get our wish about him from his father. Indeed we shall do it."

The Prophet Yusuf set up a plan. He asked his stepbrothers to go home and to return to him with their younger brother Benjamin, promising that he, Prophet Yusuf would pay them back by giving them a full measure of corn. At the same time, he told his servants to return their payment for the corn, and the servants discreetly placed it in their saddlebags. He predicted that when they find that he did not even charge them for the corn, they would be bound to return to him and ask for more.

And (Prophet Joseph) told his servants to put their stock in trade (with which they had bartered) into their saddlebags so they should know it only when they returned to their people in order that they might come back.

Now when they returned to their father they said: "O our father!" "No more measure of grain shall we get (unless we take our brother): so send our brother with us that we may get our measure; and we will indeed take every care of him."

He said: "Shall I trust you with him with any result other than when I trusted you with his brother aforetime?" But Allah is the best to take care (of him) and He is the Most Merciful of those who show mercy!

Then when they opened their baggage, they found their stock in trade (what they bartered/money) had been returned to them.

They said: "O our father!" "What (more) can we desire?" "Our stock in trade has been returned to us: so we shall get (more) food for our family; we shall take care of our brother; and add (at the same time) a full camel's load (of grain to our provisions): this is but a small quantity."

Jacob, their father said: "Never will I send him with you until ye swear a solemn oath to me in Allah's name that ye will be sure to bring him back to me unless ye are yourselves hemmed in (and made powerless)." And when they had sworn their solemn oath he said: "Over all that we say be Allah the Witness and Guardian!" Further, he said; "O my sons, enter not all by one gate: enter ye by different gates." "Not that I can profit you aught against Allah (with my advice): none can command except Allah: on Him do I put my trust and let all that trust put their trust on Him."

And when they entered in the manner their father had enjoined, it did not profit them in the least against (the Plan of) Allah: it was but a necessity of Jacob's soul that he discharged. For he was by Our instruction full of knowledge (and experience): but most men know not.

Now when they came into Joseph's presence he received his (full) brother to stay with him.

The Prophet Yusuf told his brothers the truth about himself and improvised another plan. He purposely placed the King's drinking cup in his brother Benjamin's saddlebag. When the guards shouted out that the King's cup was found missing and they searched the brothers, his brothers feared losing Benjamin and begged the King to take one of them instead. The Prophet Yusuf refused and ordered that Benjamin be taken into custody. Since the stepbrothers had promised their father, the Prophet Yaqub, that they were going to return Benjamin to him, they were afraid of what might happen to their father if they didn't.

He said (to him): "Behold!" "I am thy (own) brother; so grieve not at aught of their doings." At length when he had furnished them forth with provisions (suitable) for them he put the drinking cup into his brother's saddlebag.

Then shouted out a Crier: "O ye (in) the Caravan!" "Behold!" "Ye are thieves without doubt!"

They said turning towards them: "What is it that ye miss?"

They (the Egyptians) said: "We miss the great beaker of the king; for him who produces it is (the reward of) a camel-load; I will be bound by it."

The brothers said: "By Allah!" "Well ye know that we came not to make mischief in the land and we are no thieves!"

The Egyptians said: "What then shall be the penalty of this if ye are (proved) to have lied?" They said: "The penalty should be that he in whose saddle bag it is found should be held (as bondman) to atone for the (crime)."

Allah reveals: Thus it is we punish the wrongdoers! So he began (the search) with their baggage before (he came to) the baggage of his brother: at length He brought it out of his brother's baggage. Thus did We plan for Joseph. He could not take his brother by the law of the king except that Allah willed it (so.) We raise to degrees (of wisdom) whom We please: but over all endued with knowledge is One the All-Knowing.

They (the brothers) said: "If he steals there was a brother of his who did steal before (him)."

Allah reveals: However, these things did Joseph keep locked in his heart revealing not the secrets to them. He (simply) said (to himself): "Ye are the worse situated; and Allah knoweth best the truth of what ye assert!"

They (the brothers) said: "O exalted one!" "Behold!" "He has a father aged and venerable (who will grieve for him): so take one of us in his place: for we see that thou art (gracious) in doing good."

The Egyptians said: "Allah forbid that we take other than him with whom we found our property: indeed (if we did so) we should be acting wrongfully." Now when they saw no hope of his (yielding) they held a conference in private.

The leader among them (the brothers) said: "Know ye not that your father did take an oath from you in Allah's name and how before this ye did fail in your duty with Joseph?" "Therefore, will I not leave this land until my father permits me or Allah commands me; and He is the best to command." "Turn ye back to your father and say, 'O our father! Behold! Thy son committed theft: we bear witness only to what we know and we could not well guard against the unseen! "Ask at the town where we have been and the caravan in which we returned and (you will find) we are indeed telling the truth."

Jacob said: "Nay but ye have yourselves contrived a story (good enough) for you." Therefore, patience is most fitting (for me). Maybe Allah will bring them (back) all to me (in the end): for He is indeed full of knowledge and wisdom." And he turned away from them and said: "How great is my grief for Joseph!" And his eyes became white with sorrow and he fell into silent melancholy.

They (the brothers) said: "By Allah!" "Never wilt thou cease to remember Joseph until thou reach the last extremity of illness or until thou die!"

He (Jacob) said: "I only complain of my distraction and anguish to Allah and I know from Allah that which ye know not." "O my sons, go ye and enquire about Joseph and his brother and never give up hope of Allah's Soothing Mercy: truly no one despairs of Allah's Soothing Mercy except those who have no faith."

The brothers listened to their father and went back to Egypt.

Then when they came (back) into (Joseph's) presence they said:

"O exalted one!" "Distress has seized us and our family; we have (now) brought but scanty capital: So pay us full measure (we pray thee) and treat it as charity to us: for Allah doth reward the charitable."

He said: "Know ye how ye dealt with Joseph and his brother not knowing (what ye were doing)?" Joseph confessed the truth.

They said: "Art thou indeed Joseph?"

He said: "I am Joseph and this is my brother: Allah has indeed been gracious to us (all): behold he that is righteous and patient never will Allah suffer the reward to be lost of those who do right."

They said: "By Allah!" "Indeed has Allah preferred thee above us and we certainly have been guilty of sin!"

He said: "This day let no reproach be (cast) on you: Allah will forgive you and He is the Most Merciful of those who show mercy?" "Go with this—my shirt—and cast it over the face of my father: he will come to see (clearly). Jacob was very old and almost blind. Then come ye (here) to me together with all your family."

When the caravan left (Egypt) their father said: "I do indeed scent the presence of Joseph: nay think me not a dotard."

They said: "By Allah!" "Truly thou art in thine old wandering mind." Then when the bearer of the good news came he cast (the shirt) over his face and he forthwith regained clear sight.

He said: "Did I not say to you `Know from Allah that which ye know not?"

They said: "O our father!" "Ask for us forgiveness for our sins for we were truly at fault." He said: "Soon will I ask my Lord for forgiveness for you: for He is indeed Oft-Forgiving, Most Merciful."

Jacob and his family went to Egypt to see Joseph.

Then when they entered the presence of Joseph he provided a home for his parents with himself and said: "Enter ye Egypt (all) in safety if it please Allah." And he raised his parents high on the throne (of dignity) and they fell down in prostration (all) before him.

He (Joseph) said: "O my father!" "This is the fulfillment of my vision of old!" "Allah hath made it come true!" "He was indeed good to me when He took me out of prison and brought you (all here) out of the desert (even) after Satan had sown enmity between me and my brothers." "Verily my Lord understandeth best the mysteries of all that He planneth to do: for verily He is full of knowledge and wisdom." "O my Lord!" "Thou hast indeed bestowed on me some power and taught me something of the interpretation of dreams and events." "O Thou Creator of the heavens and the earth!" "Thou art my Protector in this world and in the Hereafter take thou my soul (at death) as one submitting to Thy Will (as a Muslim) and unite me with the righteous."

Such is one of the stories of what happened unseen, which We reveal by inspiration unto thee: nor wast thou (present) with them when they concerted their plans together in the process of weaving their plots. Yet no faith will the greater part of mankind have however ardently thou dost desire it. And no reward dost thou ask of them for this: it is no less than a Message for all creatures.[3]

The Prophet Yusuf was determined to handle all of his affairs in a peaceful, logical, and amicable manner. He understood what it took to reason and solve matters through his thoughts, feelings, dreams and intellect. His suffering and imprisonment did not drive him to lose faith and patience in the Almighty. He was determined to express himself in a way that would bring good to others and teach them that earthly greed leads to temporary pleasure and cannot compare to God's Heavenly world. His spiritual struggle or *Jihad* was beyond the best of men, and only his father and a few others knew that he was the instrument in leading mankind to divine virtuousness.

Chapter 12

Prophet Shuaib

The Medianites were descendants of Prophet Ibrahim. They were arrogant migrants and merchants who took pride in crime and cheated people of their dues by purposely mishandling the scale. They committed highway robbery and rejected religion and the belief in God.

The Prophet Shuaib's mission was to help the Medianites believe in God. He did this by reminding them that they were, at one point, an insignificant tribe who were given wealth and prosperity through God's will and therefore should at least be grateful enough to worship Him. He also reminded them of the fate of those who had turned from God in the past. Unfortunately, the Medianites ignored the Prophet Shuaib's supplications and were taken by an earthquake, hence eliminating their posterity from history.[1]

To the Madyan people We sent Shu`aib one of their own brethren…

He said: "O my people!" "Worship Allah; Ye have no other Allah but Him." "Now hath come unto you a clear (sign) from your Lord!" "Give just measure in weight (when you weigh things on a scale or do not cheat people) nor withhold from people the things that are their due; and do no mischief on the earth after it has been set in order: that will be best for you if ye have faith." "And squat not on every road breathing threats hindering from the path of Allah those who believe in Him and seeking in it something crooked; but remember how ye were little and He gave you increase." "And hold in your mind's eye what was the end of those who did mischief." "And if there is a party among you who believes in the message with which I have been sent and a party which does not believe hold yourselves in patience until Allah doth decide between us: for He is the best to decide."

The leaders of the arrogant party among his people said: "O Shu'aib!" "We shall certainly drive thee out of our city (thee) and those who believe with thee: or else ye (thou and they) shall have to return to our ways and religion."

He said: "What!" "Even though we do detest (them)?" "We should indeed invent a lie against Allah if we return to your ways after Allah hath rescued us therefrom; nor could we by any manner of means return thereto unless it is as in the Will and plan of Allah Our Lord." "Our Lord can reach out to the utmost recesses of things by His knowledge." "In Allah is our trust." "Our Lord, decide Thou between us and our people in truth for Thou art the best to decide."[2]

The Medianites urged the Prophet Shuaib and a small portion of people who believed in God to drop their faith and adopt the religion of the unbelievers and their ancestors and if they complied, they would be given a share in prosperity and wealth. The Prophet Shuaib and his followers refused the offer and were determined to believe in God and the hereafter. They knew that the unbelievers would be punished or exterminated if they refused to join them in faith, and they plead with them to no avail to be grateful for what God had given them.

"That which is left you by Allah is best for you if ye (but) believed!"

"But I am not set over you to keep watch!"

They said: "Oh Shu'aib!" "Does thy (religion of) prayer command thee that we leave off the worship which our fathers practiced or that we leave off doing what we like with our property?" "Truly thou art the one that forbeareth with faults and is right-minded!"

He said: "O my people, see ye whether I have a Clear (Sign) from my Lord and He hath given me sustenance (pure and) good as from Himself?" "I wish not in opposition to you to do that which I forbid you to do." "I only desire (your) betterment to the best of my power; and my success (in my task) can only come from Allah: in Him I trust and unto Him I look." "And O my people let not my dissent (from you) cause you to sin lest ye suffer a fate similar to that of the people of Noah or of Hud or of Salih nor are the people of Lut far off from you!" "But ask forgiveness of your Lord and turn unto Him (in repentance): for my Lord is indeed Full of mercy and loving-kindness."

They said: "O Shu'aib!" "Much of what thou sayest we do not understand!" "In fact among us we see that thou hast no strength!" "Were it not for thy family we should certainly have stoned thee!" "For thou hast among us no great position!"

He said: "O my people!" "Is then my family of more consideration with you than Allah?" "For ye cast Him away behind your backs (with contempt)." "But verily my Lord encompasseth on all sides all that ye do!" "And O my people!" "Do whatever ye can: I will do (my part): soon will ye know who it is on whom descends the Penalty of ignominy and who is a liar!" "And watch ye, for I too am watching with you!"[3]

Shu'aib continued "...Will ye not fear (Allah)?" "I am to you an apostle worthy of all trust." "So fear Allah and obey me." "No reward do I ask of you for it: my reward is only from the Lord of the Worlds." "Give just measure and cause no loss (to others by fraud)." "And weigh with scales true and upright." "And withhold not things justly due to men nor do evil in the land working mischief." "And fear Him Who created you and (Who created) the generations before (you)."

They said: "Thou art only one of those bewitched!" "Thou art no more than a mortal like us and indeed we think thou art a liar!" "Now cause a piece of the sky to fall on us if thou art truthful!"

He said: "My Lord knows best what ye do." But they rejected him. Then the punishment of a day of overshadowing gloom seized them and that was the Penalty of a Great Day. Verily in that is a Sign: but most of them do not believe. And verily thy Lord is He; the Exalted in Might, Most Merciful.[4]

The leaders the unbelievers among his people said: "If ye follow Shu`aib be sure then ye are ruined!" But the earthquake took them unawares and they lay prostrate in their homes before the morning! The men who rejected Shu`aib became as if they had never been in the homes where they had flourished. The men who rejected Shu`aib were ruined!

So Shu`aib left them saying: "O my people!" "I did indeed convey to you the messages for which I was sent by my Lord: I gave you good counsel but how shall I lament over a people who refuse to believe!"

Allah reveals: Whenever We sent a prophet to a town We took up its people in suffering and adversity in order that they might learn humility. Then We changed their suffering into prosperity until they grew and multiplied and began to say: "Our fathers (too) were touched by suffering and affluence..."

Behold! We called them to account unexpectedly while they realized not (their peril).[5] When Our decree issued We saved Shu'aib and those who believed with him by (special) Mercy from Ourselves: but the (mighty) Blast did seize the wrongdoers and they lay prostrate in their homes by the morning! As if they had never dwelt and flourished there! Ah! Behold! How the Madyan were removed (from sight) as were removed the Thamud![6]

The Prophet Shuaib tried repeatedly to invite his people to believe in God and to believe that he was no more than an Apostle who encouraged love, peace, and the worship of One God. Even though they yearned for his demise, he insisted that deliverance could only happen through the belief in God. He preached that they must not associate partners with God and that by applying true fraternity and gratefulness to their daily lives, they might generate a world of peace centered on eternal salvation. Unfortunately, it was difficult for him to establish a foundation of righteousness, absolute ethics and morality among a people who were unable to recognize his forewarnings and were doomed to be brought to ruin.

Chapter 13

Prophet Ayub—*Job*

Commentators believe that the Prophet Ayub was a prosperous man who believed in God. It is believed that he lived in what is now known as Saudi Arabia. He suffered from a number of calamities: his cattle were destroyed, his servants slain by the sword, and his family crushed under his roof, but he held fast to his faith in God. To his chagrin, he was stricken by a disease that covered his entire body with sores, causing him to feel helpless and discouraged.

Those who claimed to be his friends attributed his afflictions to sin, making the Prophet Ayub feel worse. God reminded the Prophet of His mercies upon him in the past, and the Prophet resumed his humility and accepted his fate. His physical, mental, and spiritual agony made him more pious, patient, and humble. He trusted that God would restore his health and would compensate him for his patience. He found himself in a position to accept life's sweetness and bitterness and knew that hardships were happening to him for a reason.

In the end, he was restored to prosperity, with twice as much as he had before; his brethren and friends rejoined him for he started a new family and gave life to seven sons and three daughters. He lived long enough to see four generations of descendants.[1] His patience and advocacy of peace within himself was a true example of unconditional love and happiness that transcends the realm of the ordinary mind.

Commemorate Our servant Job, "Behold he cried to his Lord:" "The Evil One has afflicted me with distress and suffering!"[2]

This is when the Prophet Ayub realizes that Iblis had afflicted him and he asked God for forgiveness.

"...Truly distress has seized me but Thou art the Most Merciful of those that are merciful."[3]

(The command was given:) "Strike with thy foot: here is (water) wherein to wash cool and refreshing and (water) to drink." "And take in thy hand a little grass and strike therewith: and break not (thy oath)." Truly, We found him full of patience and constancy: how excellent in Our service! Ever did he turn (to Us)![4]

So, We listened to him: We removed the distress that was on him and We restored his people to him and doubled their number as a Grace from Ourselves and a thing for commemoration for all who serve Us.[5]

That was the reasoning about Us which We gave to Abraham (to use) against his people: We raise whom We will degree after degree: for thy Lord is full of wisdom and knowledge. We gave him Isaac and Jacob: all (three) guided: and before him, We guided Noah, and among his progeny, David, Solomon, Job, Joseph, Moses, and Aaron: thus do We reward those who do good:[6]

(It was Our power that made) the violent (unruly) wind flow (tamely) for Solomon to his order to the land which We had blessed: for We do know all things. And of the evil ones were some who dived for him and did other work besides; and lit was

We Who guarded them. And (remember) Job when he cried to his Lord "Truly distress has seized me but Thou art the Most Merciful of those that are merciful."[7]

The Prophet Ayub was a God-fearing man. He was always grateful to God, patient and steadfast. He was generous and kind. He fed the poor and used his fortune to set slaves free. Commentators have stated that Iblis was annoyed and planned to bring the Prophet Ayub to corruption and disbelief. To show Iblis that the Prophet Ayub was a faithful and patient servant, God gave Iblis permission at the time of his distress to overpower him. Iblis tried hard to lead the Prophet Ayub to disbelieve in God since he had suffered from disease for many years, and lost his possessions and family members. The Prophet Ayub exerted a tremendous amount of patience and was ultimately able to achieve peace and harmony within his soul and among the people of his land.

Chapter 14

Prophet Zul-kifl—*Ezekiel*

Kifl is an archaic Arabic word meaning "double" or "duplicate." Not much is mentioned about him in the Qur'an or Qur'anic exegesis, and some commentators even believe that the Prophet Zul-kifl might have been a nickname. Nonetheless, he was mentioned in the Qur'an to have been among the best of men. He supported his people and created peace and justice among them.

In order to shed light on the story of the Prophet Zul-kifl below, some commentators have contended that he stands for Ezekiel in the Old Testament. Prophet Zul-kifl was against those who worshipped idols and opposed God. He encouraged those who did, to change, but they refused. As a result, some of his followers and the nonbelievers were overtaken by the Plague. Many died, while others deserted their homes to find shelter elsewhere. The Prophet Zul-kifl remained in seclusion for seven days and was devastated by what he saw upon exiting his shelter. He pled with God to intervene and bring his followers back to life. God responded to his prayers and brought them back to life.

> "And (remember) Isma'il, Idris, and Zul-kifl, all (men) of constancy and patience; We admitted them to Our mercy: for they

93

were of the righteous ones."[1]

And commemorate Our Servants Abraham, Isaac, and Jacob, possessors of Power and Vision. Verily We did choose them for a special (purpose) - proclaiming the Message of the Hereafter. They were, in Our sight, truly, of the company of the Elect and the Good. And commemorate Isma'il, Elisha, and Zul-Kifl: Each of them was of the Company of the Good.[2]

Good people, families, and nations are sometimes victims of the overall chaos and disorder created by the nonbelievers. The Prophet Zul-kifl was unsuccessful in convincing the nonbelievers to adopt orderly conduct and to believe in the Almighty. He was subject to moments of distress, contradiction, and conflict. He wanted to create peace among his people and wanted them to join him in centering their world on God. He waged war in order to eradicate the nonbelievers and cleanse the world of their blasphemy. Prior to peace within a nation, he urged them to defeat the internal forces waging evil so that, once they overcame those forces, they might have been able to reflect on living in a more unified world of peace, a world free of contradiction and conflict.

Chapter 15

Prophets Musa & Harun—
Moses & Aaron

The Prophet Musa was born in Egypt around 1200 BCE at a time when the Egyptian Pharaoh Ramzi II was enslaving and abusing the children of Israel, thus openly becoming the enemy of God. The Pharaoh had a vision that a fire had come from the direction of Jerusalem, burning everyone except for the Children of Israel. His advisors interpreted his vision to mean that a boy would be born from among the Israelites and he would overpower him and destroy his kingdom. Disturbed by the vision, he ordered his guards to kill the Israelites' newborn sons, but to spare their daughters. Once this came to be, the Israelites were dismayed by the loss of their sons and pled with the Pharaoh to have mercy upon them. The Pharaoh then chose to kill their newborn sons every other year.

The Prophet Harun, the Prophet Musa's brother, was born during the year where sons were spared, but the Prophet Musa was not. Inspired through a vision, the Prophet Musa's mother placed him in a basket and sent him down the river before his birth could become known. When the Pharaoh's concubines found his basket floating in the water, they offered it to Asiya, the Pharaoh's wife. Asiya, according to the Qur'an, is one of the very few pious women in history. God inspired her to adopt the Prophet Musa and raise him as her own. When the Prophet Musa was a young man, he witnessed an argument between a Copt (Egyptian) and a Samarian (Israelite) and exhorted the Copt to leave the Samarian alone. The Copt refused, and the Prophet Musa struck and accidentally killed him.

The next day, the Prophet Musa was warned to flee Egypt because the Pharaoh had discovered that he had killed the Copt and believed that such a crime should be punished by death. Once a fugitive, the Prophet Musa reached Madyan, situated near the Red Sea southeast of Mount Sinai, where he met the daughter of the Prophet Shuaib and eventually married her. He worked as a shepherd for the Prophet Shuaib, who entrusted his herds to him and gave him a staff to use. The staff remained with the Prophet Musa wherever he went.

One day he saw a fire and went to discover its source. This fire was created by the power of God to attract the Prophet Musa. Once in His presence, God addressed him (the only prophet to be directly spoken to by God in history) and instructed him to return to the Pharaoh to free the Israelites. Accompanied by his brother, the Prophet Harun, the Prophet Musa overcame the Pharaoh's might and brought the Israelites to freedom.[1]

> Also mentioned in the Book is the story of Moses, for he was especially chosen and he was an apostle and a prophet.[2] These are verses of the Book that make things clear.[3] Moreover We gave Moses the Book completing (Our favor) to those who would do right and explaining all things in detail and a guide and a mercy that they might believe in the meeting with their Lord.[4] Those who believe (in the Qur'an) and those who follow the Jewish (Scriptures) and the Christians and the Sabians and who believe in Allah and the last day and work righteousness shall have their reward with their Lord; on them shall be no fear nor shall they grieve.[5]

> Truly, Pharaoh elated himself in the land and broke up its people into sections depressing a small group among them, their sons he slew but he kept alive their females, for he was indeed a maker of mischief. Moreover, We wished to be gracious to those who were being depressed in the land (the Israelis) and to make them leaders

in faith and make them heirs. To establish a firm place for them in the land and to show Pharaoh, Haman, (Pharoah's minister) and their hosts (soldiers) at their hands the very things against which they were taking precautions.

Here, Pharaoh took precautions against the Israelites and began to kill them, but to his dismay, the plagues of Egypt were killing thousands of Egyptians.

Therefore, We sent this inspiration to the mother of Moses, "Suckle (thy child) but when thou hast fears about him cast him into the river but fear not nor grieve, for We shall restore him to thee and We shall make him one of Our apostles." Then the people of Pharaoh picked him up from the river. It was intended that Moses should be to them an adversary and a cause of sorrow, for Pharaoh and Haman and all their hosts were men of sin.

The wife of Pharaoh said: "(Here is) a joy of the eye for me and for thee, slay him not." "It may be that he will be of use to us or we may adopt him as a son." In addition, they perceived not (what they were doing)!

But there came to be a void in the heart of the mother of Moses, she was going almost to disclose his (case) had We not strengthened her heart (with faith) so that she might remain a (firm) believer.

And she said to the sister of (Moses): "Follow him." Then, she (the sister) watched him in the character of a stranger and they knew not and We ordained that he refused suck at first until …

Moses's sister came up and said: "Shall I point out to you the people of a house that will nourish and bring him up for you and be sincerely attached to him?" Thus did We restore him to his mother that her eye might be comforted that she might not grieve and that she might know that the promise of Allah is true, but most of them do not understand.

The Prophet Musa was probably between eighteen and thirty years of age at the time of the following incident. It might have occurred during noontide siesta, when all businesses were suspended or at night while people were usually asleep. Alternatively, he may have heard that the Israelites were oppressed and as an inmate of the Palace, he could only visit the city while secretly eluding the guards.

When he reached full age and was firmly established in life, We bestowed on him wisdom and knowledge, for thus do We reward those who do good. One day, he entered the City at a time when its people were not watching and found two men fighting, one of his own religion and the other of his foes. Now the man of his own religion appealed to him against his foe and Moses struck him (one of Pharaoh's men) with his fist and made an end of him.

The Prophet Musa did not intend to kill the Egyptian; rather he wanted him to release the Israelite. Once he realized that he had killed him, he regretted his action and prayed for God's forgiveness.

Moses said: "This is a work of Evil (Satan), for he is an enemy that manifestly misleads!" He prayed, "O my Lord!" "I have indeed wronged my soul!" "Do then forgive me?" Therefore, (Allah) forgave him, for He is the Oft-Forgiving Most Merciful. He said, "O my Lord!" "For that Thou hast bestowed Thy Grace on me never shall I be a help to those who sin!"

So he saw the morning in the City looking about in a state of fear when behold the man who had the day before sought his help called aloud for his help (again).

Moses said to him: "Thou art truly it is clear a quarrelsome fellow!"

His enemy replied: "... O Moses, is it thy intention to slay me as thou slewest a man yesterday? Thy intention is none other than to become a powerful violent man in the land and not to be one who sets things right!" Then, there came a man running from the furthest end of the City.

He said: "O Moses!" "The Chiefs are taking counsel together about thee to slay thee, so get thee away for I do give thee sincere advice." He therefore got away there from looking about in a state of fear. He (Prophet Moses) prayed, "O my Lord!" "Save me from people given to wrongdoing."[6]

After the Prophet Musa fled Egypt, he began a journey of spiritual understanding. There was something in the world of spirituality that perplexed his thoughts. Even after he had received his divine mission of prophethood, he was concerned with the obscurities of true knowledge and the paradoxes of life versus death and loss versus gain. During his long journey out of Egypt, the Prophet Musa was enlightened by the deeds and sayings of a mysterious man, one of God's chosen servants.

Behold Moses said to his attendant (lad) who accompanied him out of Egypt: "I will not give up until I reach the junction of the two seas or (until) I spend years and years in travel." Nevertheless, when they reached the Junction they forgot (about) their Fish, which took its course through the sea (straight) as in a tunnel. When they had passed on (some distance) Moses said to his attendant, "Bring us our early meal; truly we have suffered much fatigue at this (stage of) our journey."

The attendant replied: "Sawest thou (what happened) when we betook ourselves to the rock?" "I did indeed forget (about) the Fish, none but Satan made me forget to tell (you) about it, it took its course through the sea in a marvelous way!"

Moses said: "That was what we were seeking after." Therefore, they went back on their footsteps following (the path they had come). Thereafter, they found one of Our servants on whom We had bestowed Mercy from Ourselves and whom We had taught knowledge from Our own presence.

Moses said to Allah's servant: "May I follow thee on the footing that thou teach me something of the (Higher) Truth which thou hast been taught?"

Allah's servant said: "Verily thou wilt not be able to have patience with me!" "And how canst thou have patience about things about which thy understanding is not complete?"

Moses said: "Thou wilt find me if Allah so wills (truly) patient, nor shall I disobey thee in aught."

The other said: "If then thou wouldst follow me ask me no questions about anything until I myself speak to thee concerning it." So they both proceeded: until when they were in the boat he scuttled it.

Moses said: "Hast thou scuttled it in order to drown those in it?" "Truly a strange thing hast thou done!"

He answered: "Did I not tell thee that thou canst have no patience with me?"

Moses said: "Rebuke me not for forgetting nor grieve me by raising difficulties in my case." Then they proceeded, until when they met a young man he slew him.

Moses said: "Hast thou slain an innocent person who had slain none?" "Truly a foul (unheard-of) thing hast thou done!"

He answered: "Did I not tell thee that thou canst have no patience with me?"

Moses said: "If ever I ask thee about anything after this keep me not in thy company, then wouldst thou have received (full) excuse from my side." Then they proceeded, until when they came to the inhabitants of a town they asked them for food but they refused them hospitality. They found there a wall on the point of falling down but he set it up straight.

Moses said: "If thou hadst wished surely thou couldst have exacted some recompense for it!"

He answered: "This is the parting between me and thee, now will I tell thee the interpretation of (those things) over which thou wast unable to hold patience." "As for the boat it belonged to certain men in dire want, they plied on the water, I but wished to render it unserviceable for there was after them a certain king who seized on every boat by force." "As for the youth his parents were people of Faith and we feared that he would grieve them by obstinate rebellion and ingratitude (to Allah and man)." "So we desired that their Lord would give them in exchange (a son) better in purity (of conduct) and closer in affection." "As for the wall it belonged to two youths orphans in the Town; there was beneath it a buried treasure to which they were entitled, their father had been a righteous man, so thy Lord desired that they should attain their age of full strength and get out their treasure a mercy (and favor) from thy Lord." "I did it not of my own accord." "Such is the interpretation of (those things) over which thou wast unable to hold patience."[7]

*   *   *

And when he arrived at the watering (place) in Madyan, he found a group of men watering (their flocks) and besides them, he found two women who were keeping back (their flocks).

Moses said: "What is the matter with you?"

They said: "We cannot water (our flocks) until the shepherds take back (their flocks), and our father is a very old man." So he watered (their flocks) for them; then he turned back to the shade and said, "O my Lord!" "Truly am I in (desperate) need of any good that thou dost send me!" ... Afterwards one of the (damsels) came (back) to him walking bashfully.

She said: "My father invites thee that he may reward thee for having watered (our flocks) for us." So when he came to him and narrated the story ...

The father said: "Fear thou not, (well) hast thou escaped from unjust people."

Said one of the (damsels): "O my (dear) father!" "Engage him on wages, truly the best of men for thee to employ is the (man) who is strong and trusty..."

The father said: "I intended to wed one of these my daughters to thee on condition that thou serve me for eight years; but if thou complete ten years it will be (grace) from thee. But I intend not to place thee under a difficulty, thou wilt find me indeed if Allah wills one of the righteous."

Moses said: "Be that (the agreement) between me and thee, whichever of the two terms I fulfill let there be no ill-will to me." "Be Allah a witness to what we say."

When Moses had fulfilled the term and was traveling with his family, he perceived a fire in the direction of Mount Tur.

Moses said to his family: "Tarry ye; I perceive a fire; I hope to bring you from there some information or a burning firebrand that ye may warm yourselves."

When he came to the (Fire) …

A voice from the right bank of the valley from a tree in hallowed ground called out: "O Moses!" "Verily I am Allah the Lord of the Worlds …"[8] "… Therefore (in My presence) put off thy shoes, thou art in the sacred valley Tuwa." "I have chosen thee, listen then to the inspiration (sent to thee). "Verily, I am Allah, there is no Allah but I, so serve thou me (only) and establish regular prayer for celebrating My praise." "Verily the Hour is coming My design is to keep it hidden and every soul will receive its reward by the measure of its endeavor." "Therefore let not those who follow their own lusts divert thee there from lest thou perish!"[9]

God reminded Musa of his past and the favors that he had bestowed on him from the day he was born and how He had inspired his mother to float him in the river.

"… We brought thee back to thy mother that her eye might be cooled and she should not grieve." "This is when Moses's sister had informed Pharaoh's wife that she knew of someone who could suckle the infant." "Then thou didst slay a man but We saved thee from trouble and We tired thee in various ways." "Then didst thou tarry a number of years with the people of Madyan." "Then didst thou come hither as ordained O Moses!"[10]

Allah said: "I have prepared you for myself and service;[11] and what is that in thy right hand O Moses?"

Moses said: "It is my rod, on it I lean; with it I beat down fodder for my flocks; and in it I find other uses."

Allah said: "Throw it O Moses!" He threw it and behold it was a snake active in motion.[12] Now do thou throw thy rod!" But when he saw it moving (of its own accord)as if it had been a snake, he turned back in retreat, and retraced not his steps: "O Moses!" (it was said), "Fear not: truly, in My presence, those called as apostles have no fear."[13]

The Prophet Musa had dark skin, but to his astonishment when he put his hand over his chest, it turned white.

"Move thy hand into thy bosom and it will come forth white without stain (or harm) and draw thy hand close to thy side (to guard) against fear."

"Those are the two credentials from thy Lord to Pharaoh and his Chiefs, for truly they are a people rebellious and wicked."

Moses said: "O my Lord!" "I have slain a man among them and I fear lest they slay me." "And my brother Prophet Aaron he is more eloquent in speech than I, so send him with me as a helper to confirm (and strengthen) me; for I fear that they may accuse me of falsehood."

Allah said: "We will certainly strengthen thy arm through thy brother and invest you both with authority so they shall not be able to touch you, with Our Signs shall ye triumph you two as well as those who follow you."[14] "Go thou and thy brother with My Signs and slacken not either of you in keeping Me in remembrance." "Go both of you to Pharaoh for he has indeed transgressed all bounds; but speak to him mildly; perchance he may take warning or fear (Allah)."

Moses said: "Our Lord!" "We fear lest He hasten with insolence against us or lest he transgress all bounds."

Allah said: "Fear not, for I am with you, I hear and see (everything)." "So go ye both to him and say 'Verily we are apostles sent by thy Lord, send forth therefore the Children of Israel with us and afflict them not, with a Sign indeed have we come from thy Lord! And peace to all who follow guidance!'" "Verily, it has been revealed to us that the Penalty (awaits) those who reject and turn away."[15]

When Moses went to them with Our Clear Signs …

They said: "This is nothing but sorcery faked up, never did we hear the like among our fathers of old!"

Moses said: "My Lord knows best who it is that comes with guidance from Him and whose End will be best in the Hereafter, certain it is that the wrongdoers will not prosper."

Pharaoh said: "O Chiefs!" "No Allah do I know for you but myself, therefore O Haman, light me a (kiln to bake bricks) out of clay and build me a lofty palace that I may mount up to the Allah of Moses, but as far as I am concerned I think (Moses) is a liar!" And he was arrogant and insolent in the land beyond reason he and his hosts, they thought that they would not have to return to Us![16]

… Pharaoh said: "Who then O Moses is the Lord of you two?"

Moses said: "Our Lord is He Who gave to each (created) thing its form and nature and further gave (it) guidance."

Pharaoh said: "What then is the condition of previous generations?"

Moses replied: "The knowledge of that is with my Lord duly recorded, my Lord never errs nor forgets."

He Who has made for you the earth like a carpet spread out; has enabled you to go about therein by roads (and channels); and has sent down water from the sky. With it have We produced divers pairs of plants each separate from the others. Eat (for yourselves) and pasture your cattle, verily in this are Signs for men endued with understanding. From the (earth) did We create you and into it shall We return you and from it shall We bring you out once again. And We showed Pharaoh all Our Signs but he did reject and refuse.

Pharaoh said: "Hast thou come to drive us out of our land with thy magic O Moses?" "But we can surely produce magic to match thine! So make a tryst between us and thee, which we shall not fail to keep - neither we nor thou - in a place where both shall have even chances."

Moses said: "Your tryst is the Day of the Festival, and let the people be assembled when the sun is well up."[17] "… Send thou with us the Children of Israel."

Pharaoh said: "Did we not cherish thee as a child among us and didst thou not stay in our midst many years of thy life?" "And thou didst a deed of thine which (thou knowest) thou didst and thou art an ungrateful (wretch)!"

Moses said: "I did it then when I was in error." "So I fled from you (all) when I feared you; but my Lord has (since) invested me with judgment (and wisdom) and appointed me as one of the apostles." "And this is the favor with which thou dost reproach me that thou hast enslaved the Children of Israel?"

Pharaoh said: "And what is the 'Lord and Cherisher of the Worlds'?"

Moses said: "The Lord and Cherisher of the heavens and the earth and all between if ye want to be quite sure."

Pharaoh said to those around him: "Do ye not listen to what he says?" "Am I not better than this Moses who is a contemptible wretch and can scarcely express himself clearly?" "Then why are not gold bracelets bestowed on him or why come not with him angels accompanying him in procession?"

Moses said: "Your Lord and the Lord of your fathers from the beginning!"

Pharaoh said: "Truly your apostle who has been sent to you is a veritable madman!"

Moses said: "Lord of the East and the West and all between if ye only had sense!"

Pharaoh said: "If thou dost put forward any Allah other than me I will certainly put thee in prison!"

Moses said: "Even if I showed you something clear and convincing?"

Pharaoh said: "Show it then if thou tellest the truth!" So Moses threw his rod and behold it was a serpent plain for all to see! And he drew out his hand and behold it was white to all beholders!

Pharaoh said to the Chiefs around him: "This is indeed a sorcerer well-versed." "His plan is to get you out of your land by his sorcery; then what is it ye counsel?"

They said: "Keep him and his brother in suspense (for a while) and dispatch to the Cities heralds to collect and bring up to thee all our sorcerers well-versed." Then, the sorcerers got together for the appointment of a day well known And the people were told, "Are ye now assemble that we may follow the sorcerers in religion if they win?"

So when the sorcerers arrived they said to Pharaoh: "Of course shall we have a suitable reward if we win?"

Pharaoh said: "Yea and more for ye shall in that case be raised to posts nearest to my person."

Moses said to them: "Throw ye that which ye are about to throw!"

So they threw their ropes and their rods and said: "By the might of Pharaoh it is we who will certainly win!" Then Moses threw his rod when behold it straightway swallows up all the falsehoods which they fake!18

So the magicians were thrown down to prostration and said: "We believe in the Lord of Prophet Aaron and Moses."

Pharaoh said: "Believe ye in Him before I give you permission?" "Surely this must be your leader who has taught you magic!" "Be sure I will cut off your hands and feet on opposite sides and I will have you crucified on trunks of palm-trees; So shall ye know for certain which of us can give the more severe and the more lasting

Punishment!"

They said: "Never shall we regard thee as more than the Clear Signs that have come to us or than Him Who created us!" "So decree whatever thou desirest to decree, for thou canst only decree (touching) the life of this world." "For us we have believed in our Lord, may He forgive us our faults and the magic to which thou didst compel us, for Allah is Best and Most Abiding."[19]

Said the chiefs of Pharaoh's people: "Wilt thou leave Moses and his people to spread mischief in the land and to abandon thee and thy gods?"

He said: "Their male children will we slay; (only) their females will we save alive; and we have over them (power) irresistible."

Said Moses to his people: "Pray for help from Allah and (wait) in patience and constancy, for the earth is Allah's to give as a heritage to such of his servants as He pleaseth; and the end is (best) for the righteous."

They said: "We have had (nothing but) trouble both before and after thou comest to us."

Moses said: "It may be that your Lord will destroy your enemy and make you inheritors in the earth; that so He may try you by your deeds."

We punished the people of Pharaoh with years (of drought) and shortness of crops; that they might receive admonition. However, when good (times) came they said, "This is due to us; when gripped by calamity they ascribed it to evil omens connected with Moses and those with him!" Behold!" "In truth, the omens of evil are theirs in Allah's sight but most of them do not understand!"

They said to Moses: "Whatever be the signs thou bringest to work therewith the sorcery on us we shall never believe in thee."

So We sent (plagues) on them wholesale death Locusts, Lice, Frogs, and Blood: Signs openly self-explained: but they were steeped in arrogance a people given to sin.

Every time the penalty fell on them they said: "O Moses!" "On our behalf call on thy Lord in virtue of his promise to thee, if thou wilt remove the penalty from us we shall truly believe in thee and we shall send away the children of Israel with thee." But every time We removed the penalty from them according to a fixed term which they had to fulfill behold, they broke their word![20]

(Remember also) Qarun, Pharaoh, and Haman, there came to them Moses with Clear Signs but they behaved with insolence on the earth; yet they could not overreach (Us). Each one of them We seized for his crime, of them against some We sent a violent tornado (with showers of stones); some were caught by a (mighty) Blast; some We caused the earth to swallow up; and some We drowned (in the waters), it was not Allah Who injured (or oppressed) them, they injured (and oppressed) their own souls.[21]

Qarun was a wealthy Israelite who worked against his own people out of greed and was blind to the fact that he could never overreach God's might and power. Haman on the other hand, was Pharaoh's minister and advisor.

Qarun was doubtless of the people of Moses; but he acted insolently towards them. Such were the treasures We had bestowed on him that their very keys would have been a burden to a body of strong men.

Behold his people said to him: "Exult not for Allah loveth not those who exult (in riches)." "But seek with the (wealth) which Allah has bestowed on thee the Home of the Hereafter nor forget thy portion in this world, but do thou good as Allah has been good to thee and seek not (occasions for) mischief in the land, for Allah loves not those who do mischief."

He (Qarun) said: "This has been given to me because of a certain knowledge which I have."

Did he not know that Allah had destroyed before him (whole) generations, which were superior to him in strength and greater in amount (of riches), they had collected? However, the wicked are not called (immediately) to account for their sins. Therefore, he went forth among his people in the (pride of his worldly) glitter.

Said those whose aim is the Life of this World: "Oh that we had the like of what Qarun has got!" "For he is truly a lord of mighty good fortune."

But those who had been granted (true) knowledge said: "Alas for you!" "The reward of Allah (in the Hereafter) is best for those who believe and work righteousness, but this none shall attain save those who steadfastly persevere (in good)." Then We caused the earth to swallow him up and his house; and he had not (the least little) party to help him against Allah nor could he defend himself.[22]

God is not pleased with men who boast their wealth like Qarun. Qarun believed that the reason he was wealthy was because he had knowledge. God showed him otherwise: wealth is for service, not for hoarding or show. In the midst of his pride, and through the power of God, Qarun was consumed by the earth. God used him as an example for those who prefer the riches of this life over hereafter.

By inspiration We told Moses: "Travel by night with My servants; for surely ye shall be pursued."

Then Pharaoh sent heralds to (all) the Cities (saying): "These (Israelites) are but a small band and they are raging furiously against us, but we are a multitude amply fore-warned." We expelled them from gardens springs treasures and every kind of honorable position; thus it was but We made the Children of Israel inheritors of such things. They pursued them at sunrise.

When the two bodies saw each other the people of Moses said: "We are sure to be overtaken." "… By no means!" "My Lord is with me!" "Soon will He guide me!"

Then We told Moses by inspiration: "Strike the sea with thy rod." Therefore, it divided and each separate part become like the huge firm mass of a mountain. And We made the other party approach thither. We delivered Moses and all who were with him; but We drowned the others. Verily in this is a Sign, but most of them do not believe. Verily thy Lord is He the Exalted in Might Most Merciful.[23] We divided them into twelve tribes or nations.

We directed Moses by inspiration when his (thirsty) people asked him for water: "Strike the rock with thy staff." And out of it there gushed forth twelve springs, each group knew its own place for water. We gave them the shade of clouds and sent down to them manna and quails (saying), "Eat of the good things We have provided for you." However, they rebelled. To Us they did no harm but they harmed their own souls. Remember it was said to them, "Dwell in this town and eat therein as ye wish but say the word of humility and enter the gate in a posture of humility; We shall forgive you your faults; We shall increase (the portion of) those who do good."

However, the transgressors among them changed the word from

that which had been given them; so We sent on them a plague from heaven for that they repeatedly transgressed. Ask them concerning the town standing close by the sea. Behold! They transgressed in the matter of the Sabbath. For on the day of their Sabbath their fish did come to them openly holding up their heads but on the day they had no Sabbath they came not, thus did We make a trial of them for they were given to transgression.

When some of them said: "Why do ye preach to a people whom Allah will destroy or visit with a terrible punishment?"

Said the preachers: "To discharge our duty to your Lord and perchance they may fear him." When they disregarded the warnings that had been given them We rescued those who forbade evil; but We visited the wrong-doers with a grievous punishment because they were given to transgression. When in their insolence they transgressed (all) prohibition

We said to them: "Be ye apes despised and rejected."

When We shook the mount over them as if it had been a canopy and they thought it was going to fall on them ... "Hold firmly to what We have given you and bring (even) to remembrance what is therein; perchance ye may fear Allah."[24] ... They came upon a people devoted entirely to (the worship) of some idols they had.

They said: "O Moses!" "Fashion for us a god like unto the gods they have."

Moses said: "Surely ye are a people without knowledge." "As to these folk the cult they are in is (but) a fragment of a ruin and vain is the (worship) which they practice." He said, "Shall I seek for you a god other than the (true) Allah when it is Allah who hath endowed you with gifts above the nations?"

And remember We rescued you from Pharaoh's people who afflicted you with the worst of penalties who slew your male children and saved alive your females, in that was a momentous trial from your Lord. We appointed for Moses thirty nights and completed (the period) with ten (more), thus was completed the term (of communion) with his Lord forty nights.

And Moses had charged his brother Aaron (before he went up): "Act for me amongst my people, do right and follow not the way of those who do mischief." When Moses came to the place appointed by Us and his Lord addressed him …

Moses said: "O my Lord!" "Show (Thyself) to me that I may look upon thee."

Allah said: "By no means canst thou see Me (direct); but look upon the mount; if it abide in its place then shalt thou see Me." When his Lord manifested his glory on the mount He made it as dust and Prophet Moses fell down in a swoon.

When Moses recovered his senses he said: "Glory be to Thee!" "To thee I turn in repentance and I am the first to believe."

Allah said: "O Moses!" I have chosen thee above (other) men by the mission I (have given thee) and the words I (have spoken to thee), take then the (revelation) which I give thee and be of those who give thanks." … And We ordained laws for him in the tablets in all matters both commanding and explaining all things (and said), "Take and hold these with firmness and enjoin thy people to hold fast by the best in the precepts, soon shall I show you the homes of the wicked (how they lie desolate)." Those who behave arrogantly on the earth in defiance of right, I will turn them away from My signs. They will not believe in them; and if they see the way of right conduct, they will not adopt it; but if they see the way of error, they will adopt it. For they rejected Our signs and failed to take warning from them. Those who reject Our signs and the meeting in the hereafter, vain are their deeds. Can they expect to be rewarded except as they have wrought?[25]

Verily in this, there are Signs for such as are firmly patient and constant grateful and appreciative.

… Moses said to his people: "Call to mind the favor of Allah to you when He delivered you from the people of Pharaoh." "They set you hard tasks and punishments slaughtered your sons and let your womenfolk live, therein was a tremendous trial from your Lord."

"And remember your Lord caused to be declared (publicly)!" "If ye are grateful, I will add more (favors) unto you; but if ye show ingratitude truly My punishment is terrible indeed." "… If ye show ingratitude ye and all on earth together—yet is Allah Free of all wants Worthy of all praise."[26] … We divided the sea for you and saved you and drowned Pharaoh's people within your very sight.

… We appointed forty nights for Moses and in his absence you took the calf (for worship) and ye did grievous wrong. Even then, We did forgive you; there was a chance for you to be grateful… We gave Moses the Scripture and the criterion (between right and wrong) there was a chance for you to be guided aright.[27]

*   *   *

When Moses was up on the mount, Allah said: "What made thee hasten in advance of thy people O Moses?"

Moses replied: "Behold they are close on my footsteps, I hastened to Thee O my Lord to please Thee."

Allah said, "We have tested thy people in thy absence, the Samiri has led them astray." "So Moses returned to his people in state of indignation and sorrow."

Samiri was an Egyptian Hebrew who led his people astray and appears to be responsible for suggesting the making of the golden calf.

Moses said: "O my people!" "Did not your Lord make a handsome promise to you?" "Did then the promise seem to you long (in coming)?" "Or did ye desire that Wrath should descend from your Lord on you and so ye broke your promise to me?"

They said: "We broke not the promise to thee as far as lay in our power, but we were made to carry the weight of the ornaments of the (whole) people and we threw them (into the fire) and that was what the Samiri suggested." "Then, he brought out (of the fire) before the (people) the image of a calf, it seemed to low ...

... so they said: "This is your god (the god of Moses), but Moses has forgotten!"

Could they not see that it could not return them a word (for answer) and that it had no power either to harm them or to do them good? Prior to this,

Aaron had already, before this said to them: "O my people!" "Ye are being tested in this, for verily your Lord is (Allah) Most Gracious, so follow me and obey my command."

They had said: "We will not abandon this cult but we will devote ourselves to it until Prophet Moses returns to us."

Moses said: "O Prophet Aaron!" "What kept thee back when thou sawest them going wrong from following me?" "Didst thou then disobey my order?"

Aaron replied: "O son of my mother!" "Seize (me not) by my beard nor by (the hair of) my head!" "Truly I feared lest thou shouldst say 'Thou hast caused a division among the Children of Israel and thou didst not respect my word!'"

Moses said: "What then is thy case O Samiri?"

Aaron replied: "I saw what they saw not, so I took a handful (of dust) from the footprint of the Apostle and threw it (into the calf), thus did my soul suggest to me."

Moses said to his people: "Get thee gone!" "But thy (punishment) in this life will be that thou wilt say 'Touch me not'; and moreover (for a future penalty) thou hast a promise that will not fail, now look at thy god of whom thou hast become a devoted worshipper, we will certainly (melt) it in a blazing fire and scatter it broadcast in the sea!" "But the god of you all is the One Allah; there is no god but He, all things He comprehends in His knowledge."[28] "... O my people!" "Ye have indeed wronged yourselves by your worship of the calf so turn (in repentance) to your Maker and slay yourselves (the wrong-doers); that will be better for you in the sight of your Maker." Then He turned toward you (in forgiveness); for He is Oft-returning Most Merciful.[29]

...And remember ye said, "O Moses!" "We shall never believe in thee until we see Allah manifestly;" but ye were dazed with thunder and lightning even as ye looked on. Then, We raised you up after your death; ye had the chance to be grateful. And We gave You the shade of clouds and sent down to you manna and quails instructing you to eat of the good things We have provided for you; (but they rebelled); to Us they did no harm but they harmed their own souls. And remember We said, "Enter this town and eat of the plenty therein as ye wish; but enter the gate with humility in posture and in words and We shall forgive you your faults and increase (the portion of) those who do good." But the transgressors changed the word from that which had been given them; so We sent on the transgressors a plague from heaven for that they infringed (our command) repeatedly. And remember Moses prayed for water for his people; We said, "Strike the rock with thy rod." Then twelve springs gushed forth. Each group knew its own place for water. So eat and drink of the sustenance provided by Allah and do neither evil nor mischief on the (face of the) earth. And remember ye said, "O Moses!" "We cannot endure one kind of food (always); so beseech thy Lord for us to produce for us of what the earth groweth its pot-herbs and cucumbers its garlic lentils and onions." He said, "Will ye exchange the better for the worse?" "Go ye down to any town and ye shall find what ye want!" They were covered with humiliation and misery; they drew on themselves the wrath of Allah ...[30]

And remember We took your covenant and We raised above you (the towering height) of Mount (Sinai) (saying), "Hold firmly to what We have given you and bring (ever) to remembrance what is therein perchance ye may fear Allah." But ye turned back thereafter had it not been for the Grace and Mercy of Allah to you ye had surely been among the lost. And well ye knew those amongst you who transgressed in the matter of the Sabbath; We said to them, "Be ye apes despised and rejected." So We made it an example to their own time and to their posterity and a lesson to those who fear Allah.

... Moses said to his people: "Allah commands that ye sacrifice a heifer."

They said: "Makest thou a laughing-stock of us?"

Moses said: "Allah save me from being an ignorant (fool)!"

They said: "Beseech on our behalf thy Lord to make plain to us what (heifer) it is!"

Moses said: "He says the heifer should be neither too old nor too young but of middling age; now do what ye are commanded!"

They said: "Beseech on our behalf thy Lord to make plain to us her color."

Moses said: "He says a fawn-colored heifer pure and rich in tone the admiration of beholders!"

They said: "Beseech on our behalf thy Lord to make plain to us what she is to us are all heifers alike; we wish indeed for guidance if Allah wills."

Moses said: "He says a heifer not trained to till the soil or water the fields; sound and without blemish."

They said: "Now hast thou brought the truth." Then they offered her in sacrifice but not with good-will.

Remember ye slew a man and fell into a dispute among yourselves as to the crime but Allah was to bring forth what ye did hide.

Therefore, We said: "Strike the (body) with a piece of the (heifer)." Thus Allah bringeth the dead to life and showeth you His Signs perchance ye may understand. Thenceforth were your hearts hardened; they became like a rock and even worse in hardness. For among rocks there are some, from which rivers gush forth; others there are which when split asunder send forth water; and others, which sink for fear of Allah. And Allah is not unmindful of what ye do.[31]

They said: "O Moses!" "In this land are a people of exceeding strength, never shall we enter it until they leave it, if (once) they leave then shall we enter."

(But) among (their) Allah-fearing men were two on whom Allah had bestowed His Grace...

They said: "Assault them at the (proper) gate, when once ye are in, victory will be yours. But in Allah put your trust if ye have faith. "O Moses!" "While they remain there never shall we be able to enter to the end of time." "Go thou and thy Lord and fight ye two while we sit here (and watch)."

Moses said: "O my Lord!" "I have power only over myself and my bother so separate us from this rebellious people!"

Allah said: "Therefore will the land be out of their reach for forty years; in distraction will they wander through the land, but sorrow thou not over these rebellious people."[32]

In the past, We granted to Moses and Prophet Aaron the Criterion (for judgment) and a Light and a Message for those who would do right.[33]

O ye Children of Israel, We delivered you from your enemy and We made a Covenant with you on the side of Mount (Sinai) and We sent down to you Manna and quails, (Saying), Eat of the good things We have provided for your sustenance but commit no excess therein lest My Wrath should justly descend on you, and those on whom descends My Wrath do perish indeed! But without doubt I am (also) He that forgives again and again to those who repent believe and do right who in fine are ready to receive true guidance.[34] Would ye question your Apostle as Moses was questioned of old? However, whoever changeth from faith to unbelief hath strayed without doubt from the even way.[35]

… We sent Moses with Our Clear (Signs) and an authority manifest unto Pharaoh and his Chiefs, but they followed the command of Pharaoh and the command of Pharaoh was no right (guide). He will go before his people on the Day of Judgment and lead them into the Fire (as cattle are led to water), but woeful indeed will be this leading (and) the place led to![36]

And Allah sets forth as an example to those who believe the wife of Pharaoh (Asiyah),

Behold she said: "O my Lord!" "Build for me in nearness to Thee a mansion in the Garden and save me from Pharaoh and his doings and save me from those that do wrong."[37]

Of some Apostles, We have already told thee the story; of others, We have not; and to Moses Allah spoke direct.[38] Let the people of the Gospel Judge by what Allah hath revealed therein. If any do fail to judge by (the light of) what Allah hath revealed they are (no better than) those who rebel.[39] And Pharaoh and those before him and the cities overthrown committed habitual sin and disobeyed (each) the apostle of their Lord; so He punished them with an abundant Penalty.[40]

The Prophet Musa's curiosity about life's mysteries along with his frustration toward the injustices of the Pharaoh and his followers led him to pursue his own mission and take matters in his own hand. He yearned for peace and equality between the Egyptians and the Hebrews, and could not control his emotions in the face of ill treatment of the oppressed. He fled Egypt with hope to find peace elsewhere. God chose him to be His prophet and spoke to him. After talking to God and connecting with Him emotionally and spiritually, he seized the power He had bestowed on him and returned to the Pharaoh and requested that he share in his beliefs and convictions in the existence of God. The Prophet Musa solicited the obstinate Pharaoh who was unconvinced of his message to at least free the Israelites so that he may guide them toward salvation. The Pharaoh's deceiving ploy against the Prophet Musa was prevented through God's miracles allowing the Pharaoh himself to believe in God before he died and the Prophet Musa to increase his credibility in God's power. In the end, he hoped that, by centering on God, all of his people would be able to enjoy perpetual freedom, peace, and supreme happiness.

Chapter 16

Prophet Dawood—*David*

The Prophet Dawood was not only a shepherd, a warrior, a king, and a prophet, but he was endowed with intelligence and exceptional strength. For even as a young man, he slew the Philistine giant Goliath. The story below gives clarity to this matter.

> Hast thou not turned thy vision to the chiefs of the children of Israel after (the time of) Moses?

> They said to a Prophet among them: "Appoint for us a king that we may fight in the cause of Allah…"[1]

At the time, Israel was suffering from corruption and had been defeated by the Philistines. They also lost the Ark of the Covenant (a chest of acacia wood, covered and lined with pure gold) to the enemy who retained it for seven months and ultimately found no need for it. The Ark was believed to contain the "testimony of God" or the Hebraic Scriptres engraved in stone with relics of the Prophet Musa and the Prophet Harun. It remained for about twenty years in the *qarya* (village) of *Yaarim* or *Kirjath-jearim* located around the land of the Philistines. The Ark of the Covenant was essentially a symbol of peace, unity, and authority. Ultimately, the people pressed Samuel to appoint them a king who might cure them of their ills. Even though Samuel knew that the people were indecisive and were acting out of self-interest, he appointed Talut to be their king. Unfortunately, they failed to seek God's reverence and neither the king nor the Ark was a means to help them transform their kingdom into one of peace and harmony.[2]

He (Samuel) said: "...Is it not possible if ye were commanded to fight that ye will not fight?"

They said: "How could we refuse to fight in the cause of Allah seeing that we were turned out of our homes and our families?"

But when they were commanded to fight they turned back except a small band among them. Nevertheless, Allah has full knowledge of those who do wrong.

Their Prophet (Samuel) said to them: "Allah hath appointed Talut as king over you."

They said: "How can he exercise authority over us when we are better fitted than he to exercise authority and he is not even gifted with wealth in abundance?"

Samuel said: "Allah hath chosen him above you and hath gifted him abundantly with knowledge and bodily prowess; Allah granteth His authority to whom He pleaseth. Allah careth for all and He knoweth all things."

And (further) their Prophet said to them: "A sign of his authority is that there shall come to you the Ark of the Covenant with (an assurance) therein of security from your Lord and the relics left by the family of Musa and the family of Prophet Harun carried by angels." In this is a Symbol for you if ye indeed have faith.

When Talut set forth with the armies he said: "Allah will test you at the stream; if any drinks of its water he goes not with my army; only those who taste not of it go with me; a mere sip out of the hand is excused." But they all drank of it except a few.

When they crossed the river he and the faithful ones with him they said: "This day we cannot cope with Goliath and his forces."

However, those who were convinced that they must meet Allah said: "How oft by Allah's will hath a small force vanquished a big one?" Allah is with those who steadfastly persevere. When they advanced to meet Goliath and his forces they prayed, "Our Lord!" "Pour out constancy on us and make our steps firm; help us against those that reject faith." By Allah's will they routed them, and David slew Goliath; and Allah gave him power and wisdom and taught him whatever (else) He willed. In addition, if Allah did not check one set of people by means of another, the earth would indeed be full of mischief but Allah is full of bounty to all the worlds?[3]

The Prophet Dawood's story in the Qur'an demonstrates that numbers do not count. It is faith, determination, and the blessings of God that outweigh everything else. If God is with us, the enemy's weapon may become an instrument of his or her own destruction. God's plan is universal. He loves and protects all those who believe in Him, and we must never lose faith in His compassion.[4]

That was the reasoning about Us which We gave to Abraham (to use) against his people: We raise whom We will degree after degree: for thy Lord is full of wisdom and knowledge. We gave him Isaac and Jacob: all (three) We guided: and before him We guided Noah and among his progeny David, Solomon, Jacob, Yusuf, Musa, and Prophet Harun: thus do We reward those who do good.[5]

And remember David and Solomon when they gave judgment in the matter of the field into which the sheep of certain people had strayed by night: We did witness their judgment.[6]

Thus the sheep, on account of the negligence of its shepherd, entered a cultivated field (or vineyard) by night and ate the crops causing a year's worth of damage. As king, the Prophet Dawood considered the matter seriously and awarded the sheep to the owner of the field in compensation for the damage. His eleven-year-old son the Prophet Suleiman believed that the penalty would be better if the crime fit the offence. The loss was the loss of the fruits; the property itself, was not lost. The Prophet Suleiman suggested that the owner of the vineyard should not take the sheep. He believed that he should detain them long enough to recover the actual damage. By this, he could use the milk, wool, and possibly the newborn offspring and then return the sheep to the shepherd. The Prophet Dawood consented to his young son's suggestion. Clearly, God must have inspired the young boy and his father was wise enough to realize that God was watching over him at all times.[7]

Have patience at what they say and remember Our Servant David the man of strength: for he ever turned (to Allah). It was We that made the hills declare in unison with him Our Praises at eventide and at break of day. And the birds gathered (in assemblies): all with him did turn (to Allah). We strengthened his kingdom and gave him wisdom and sound judgment in speech and decision.[8]

…But those who were convinced that they must meet Allah said: "How oft by Allah's will hath a small force vanquished a big one? Allah is with those who steadfastly persevere." When they advanced to meet Goliath and his forces they prayed: "Our Lord!" "Pour out constancy on us and make our steps firm; help us against those that reject faith." By Allah's will they routed them: and David slew Goliath; and Allah gave him power and wisdom and taught him whatever (else) He willed. David used his shepherd sling to knock Goliath down and slay him.) And did not Allah check one set of people by means of another the earth would indeed be full of mischief but Allah is full of bounty to all the worlds. These are the signs of Allah; We rehearse them to thee in truth: verily thou (Prophet Muhammad *pbuh*) art one of the apostles.[9]

Has the Story of the Disputants reached thee? Behold they climbed over the wall of the private chamber; When they entered the presence of David and he was terrified of them ...

They said: "Fear not: We are two disputants one of whom has wronged the other: decide now between us with truth and treat us not with injustice but guide us to the even Path." "This man is my brother; he has nine and ninety ewes and I have (but) one: Yet he says 'Commit her to my care' and is (moreover) harsh to me in speech."

David said: "He has undoubtedly wronged thee in demanding thy (single) ewe to be added to his (flock of) ewes: truly many are the Partners (in business) who wrong each other: not so do those who believe and work deeds of righteousness and how few are they?"

... And David gathered that We had tried him: he asked forgiveness of his Lord fell down bowing (in prostration) and turned (to Allah in repentance). Therefore, We forgave him this (lapse): he enjoyed indeed a Near Approach to Us and a beautiful place of (final) Return. O David! We did indeed make thee a vicegerent on earth: so judge thou between men in truth (and justice): nor follow thou the lusts (of thy heart) for they will mislead thee from the Path of Allah: for those who wander astray from the Path of Allah is a Penalty Grievous for that they forget the Day of Account.[10]

Such are Our Bounties: whether thou bestow them (on others) or withhold them no account will be asked. And he enjoyed indeed a Near Approach to Us and a beautiful Place of (final) Return.[11]

By observing the stories that transpired over the lifetime of the Prophet Dawood, Muslims conclude that only God has the power to guide toward a more unified world of peace and eternal prosperity. If the Prophet Dawood were able to sway the most powerful of men, it goes to demonstrate that God's power and miracles are behind the test of faith. God is powerful, loving, and absolute. His love for man and the examples that He has set forth through the lives of His prophets should be the source of energy that guides mankind to believe in Him and in the afterlife. God urges men to live in peace, a kind of peace that starts from within so that they may ultimately trust in His salvation rather than worthlessly exhaust their efforts in expanding material wealth and prosperity. The story of the Prophet Dawood teaches us to preserve our national existence and faith with courage and firmness.

Chapter 17

Prophet Suleiman—*Solomon*

God granted to the Prophet Suleiman the intelligence and the faculties by which he could tame the more unruly forces of nature. He was a great and righteous king who served God and turned to him in every instance. He owned many horses and could have used his power and wealth in ways that did not illustrate his devotion to God and to prayer, but he did not. Rather, he used it over men and the forces of nature so that he could remain devoted to God in mind and in spirit.[1] He lived a life of joy, satisfaction, free will, and peace. He set the example for others to live in peace and harmony and he knew that life was a test of faith and that without believing and trusting in God, life would be meaningless.

To David We gave Solomon (for a son) how excellent in Our service! Ever did he turn (to Us)! Behold there were brought before him at eventide coursers (swift horse) of the highest breeding; and swift of foot;

And he said: "Truly do I love the love of Good with a view to the glory of my Lord until (the sun) was hidden in the veil (of Night)."

The Prophet Suleiman's love of horses was highly spiritual, yet he never neglected his evening prayers. He always returned to admire his horses after sunset.

"Bring them back to me." Then he began to pass his hand over (their) legs and their necks."

And We did try Solomon: We placed on his throne a body without life: but he did turn to Us in true devotion:

He had everything, but felt that he had nothing unless he devoted himself and his spirit to God.

Solomon said: "O my Lord!" "Forgive me and grant me a Kingdom which (it may be) suits not another after me: for Thou art the Grantor of Bounties (without measure)."

He wanted to show God that he was different from others and that he would not abuse the power granted him. God bestowed immeasurable powers and bounties on the Prophet Suleiman, and he was free to give away anything he liked or keep anything he liked. Any ordinary man would have been tempted to abuse such power, but the Prophet Suleiman used it legally and ethically.

Then We subjected the Wind to his power to flow gently to his order whithersoever he willed, as also the evil ones (including) every kind of builder and diver, as also others bound together in fetters.[2]

This has been interpreted to mean that God gave the Prophet Suleiman miraculous power over the winds.

And when came to them an Apostle from Allah confirming what was with them a party of the people of the Book threw away the Book of Allah behind their backs as if (it had been something) they did not know! They followed what the evil ones gave out (falsely) against the power of Solomon; the blasphemers were not Solomon but the evil ones teaching men magic and such things as came down at Babylon to the angels Harut and Marut. But neither of these taught anyone (such things) without saying: "We are only on trial, so do not blaspheme." They learned from them the means to sow discord between man and wife. But they could not thus harm anyone except by Allah's permission. And they learned what harmed them not what profited them. And they knew that the buyers of (magic) would have no share in the happiness of the Hereafter. And vile was the price for which they did sell their souls if they but knew! If they had kept their faith and guarded themselves from evil far better had been the reward from their Lord if they but knew![3]

God had given the Prophet Suleiman great powers, but the nonbelievers (especially those who performed magic), tried to harm him.

To Solomon We inspired the (right) understanding of the matter: to each (of them) We gave Judgment and Knowledge; it was Our power that made the hills and the birds celebrate Our praises with David: it was We Who did (these things). It was We Who taught him the making of coats of mail for your benefit to guard you from each other's violence: will ye then be grateful? (It was Our power that made) the violent (unruly) wind flow (tamely) for Solomon to his order to the land which We had blessed: for We do know all things. And of the evil ones were some who dived for him and did other work besides; and lit was We Who guarded them.[4]

Obviously, God granted him such intelligence. This is in reference to Palestine, the Prophet Suleiman's capital, though his influence extended toward northern Syria.

The Prophet Suleiman also tamed the *Jinn* or spirits with Wisdom. It was common practice at that time for people to have discussions with the *Jinn*.

We gave (in the past) knowledge to David and Solomon: and they both said: "Praise be to Allah Who has favored us above many of His servants who believe!" And Solomon was David's heir.

Solomon said: "O ye people!" "We have been taught the speech of Birds and on us has been bestowed (a little) of all things: this is indeed Grace manifest (from Allah)." And before Solomon were marshaled his hosts of Jinn and men and birds and they were all kept in order and ranks.

The Prophet Suleiman was bestowed the power to understand the language of birds and ants, which in turn gave him the power to control and respect the smallest to the largest of creatures.

At length when they came to a (lowly) valley of ants one of the ants said: "O ye ants get into your habitations lest Solomon and his hosts crush you (under foot) without knowing it."

Solomon smiled amused at her speech and said: "O my Lord!" "So order me that I may be grateful for Thy favors which Thou hast bestowed on me and on my parents and that I may work the righteousness that will please Thee: and admit me by Thy Grace to the ranks of Thy righteous Servants."

The Prophet Suleiman was amused and declared his gratitude to God after hearing the conversation between the ants. He also spoke with the birds who appeared to be forever at his service.

Solomon said: "Why is it I see not the Hoopoe?" "Or is he among the absentees?" "I will certainly punish him with a severe Penalty or execute him unless he bring me a clear reason (for absence)." But the Hoopoe tarried not far:

Hoopoe said: "I compassed (territory) which thou hast not compassed and I have come to thee from Saba with tidings true." "I found (there) a woman ruling over them and provided with every requisite; and she has a magnificent throne. "I found her and her people worshipping the sun besides Allah. Satan has made their deeds seem pleasing in their eyes and has kept them away from the Path so they receive no guidance (Kept them away from the Path) that they should not worship Allah Who brings to light what is hidden in the heavens and the earth and knows what ye hide and what ye reveal." "Allah!" "There is no Allah but He! Lord of the Throne Supreme!"

Solomon said: "Soon shall we see whether thou hast told the truth or lied!" "Go thou with this letter of mine and deliver it to them: then draw back from them and (wait to) see what answer they return …"

The Queen said: "Ye chiefs!" "Here is delivered to me a letter worthy of respect." "It is from Solomon and is (as follows): In the name of Allah Most Gracious Most Merciful: be ye not arrogant against me but come to me in submission to the true Religion." "… Ye chiefs!" "Advise me in (this) my affair: no affair have I decided except in your presence."

They said: "We are endued with strength and given to vehement war: but the command is with thee; so consider what thou wilt command."

She said: "Kings when they enter a country despoil it and make the noblest of its people its meanest: thus do they behave." "But I am going to send him a present and (wait) to see with what (answer) return (my) ambassadors."

How when (the embassy) came to Solomon he said: "Will ye give me abundance in wealth?" "But that which Allah has given me is better than that which He has given you! Nay it is ye who rejoice in your gift!" "Go back to them and be sure we shall come to them with such hosts as they will never be able to meet: we shall expel them from there in disgrace and they will feel humbled (indeed)."

Solomon said (to his own men): "Ye Chiefs!" "Which of you can bring me her throne before they come to me in submission?"

Said an Ifrit of the Jinn: "I will bring it to thee before thou rise from thy Council: indeed I have full strength for the purpose and may be trusted."

Said one who had knowledge of the Book: "I will bring it to thee within the twinkling of an eye!"

Then when (Solomon) saw it placed firmly before him he said: "This is by the grace of my Lord!" "To test me whether I am grateful or ungrateful!" "And if any is grateful truly his gratitude is (a gain) for his own soul; but if any is ungrateful truly my Lord is Free of All Needs Supreme in Honor!"

Solomon said: "Transform her throne out of all recognition by her: let us see whether she is guided (to the truth) or is one of those who receive no guidance." So when she arrived she was asked "Is this thy throne?"

She said: "It was just like this; and knowledge was bestowed on us in advance of this and we have submitted to Allah (in Islam)." And he diverted her from the worship of others besides Allah: for she was (sprung) of a people that had no faith. She was asked to enter that lofty Palace: but when she saw it she thought it was a lake of water and she (tucked up her skirts) uncovering her legs.

Solomon said: "This is but a palace paved smooth with slabs of glass."

She said: "O my Lord!" "I have indeed wronged my soul: I do (now) submit (in Islam) with Solomon to the Lord of the Worlds."[5]

The Hoopoe, a beautiful bird, explained to the Prophet Suleiman that it was late because it had seen the Queen of Sheba (the woman who ruled the ancient kingdom of Sheba) and her people worshipping the sun. To see if the bird was telling the truth, the Prophet Suleiman sent it back with a letter asking the queen to worship God. Not knowing what to do, the queen questioned her council and tried to bribe the Prophet Suleiman with wealth. He refused, knowing that God would transfer her throne to him. Once this happened, she visited the Prophet Suleiman, and to her surprise, he had her throne. She immediately surrendered her will to God and to the Prophet Suleiman's religion.[6]

> And to Solomon (We made) the Wind (obedient): its early morning (stride) was a month's (journey) and its evening (stride) was a month's (journey);

The winds could cover in a short morning or evening's flight a distance that would take many days to cover by foot.

> And We made a Font of molten brass to flow for him; and there were Jinn that worked in front of him by the leave of his Lord and if any of them turned aside from Our command We made Him taste of the Penalty of the Blazing Fire. They worked for him as he desired (making) Arches Images Basins as large as Reservoirs and (cooking) Cauldrons fixed (in their places): "Work ye sons of David with thanks!" But few of My servants are grateful! Then when We decreed (Solomon's) death nothing showed them his death except a little worm of the earth which kept (slowly) gnawing away at his staff: so when he fell down the Jinn saw plainly that if they had known the unseen they would not have tarried in the humiliating Penalty (of their Task).

> There was for Saba aforetime (a beautiful city in Yemen) a Sign in their homeland two Gardens to the right and to the left. Allah gave the people of Saba wealth and sustenance as long as they remained grateful and worshipped Him. Eat of the Sustenance (provided) by your Lord and be grateful to Him: a territory fair and happy and a Lord Oft-Forgiving!" But they turned away (from Allah) and We sent against them the flood (released) from the Dams and We converted their two Garden (rows) into "gardens" producing

bitter fruit and tamarisks and some few (stunted) Lute trees. That was the Requital We gave them because they ungratefully rejected Faith: and never do We give (such) requital except to such as are ungrateful rejecters.

God is quick to punish those who are ungrateful and who refuse to believe in Him.

Between them (the Saba) and the Cities on which We had poured Our blessings We had placed Cities in prominent positions and between them We had appointed stages of journey in due proportion: "Travel therein secure by night and by day."

But they said: "Our Lord!" "Place longer distances between our journey-stages."

They became greedy and asked God to help them monopolize most of the stations in which travelers purchase their goods.

But they wronged themselves (therein). At length We made them as a tale (that is told) and We dispersed them all in scattered fragments.

Verily in this are Signs for every (soul that is) patiently constant and grateful. And on them did Satan prove true his idea and they followed him all but a Party that believed.

This is a reminder of man's "freedom of choice" and reinforces the notion that many people chose to follow Iblis's ways.

But he had no authority over them except that We might test the man who believes in the Hereafter from him who is in doubt concerning it: and thy Lord doth watch over all things.[7]

Society in general does not believe that it is possible for anyone to comprehend the language of animals and insects, yet God has repeatedly demonstrated through His prophets that He and only He is capable of creating miracles beyond man's comprehension. He gave the Prophet Suleiman the power to converse with birds and insects so that we may learn that there can be peace not only among people but among all of God's creation. The Prophet Suleiman also interacted with the *Jinn* and that ultimately helped him convey the message of Islam to the Queen of Sheba and her people who worshipped the sun. She submitted her will to God and realized that He was a power beyond anyone's comprehension. In the end, even though the Prophet Suleiman's earthly kingdom went to pieces after his death, his devotion to creating peace among his people led to the longevity of his fame.

Chapter 18

Prophet Elias—*Elijah*

The Prophet Elias was among "the Righteous," and God held him in high rank. He lived during the reign of Ahab (896–874 BCE) and Ahaziah (874–872 BCE), kings of the (northern) kingdom of Israel or Samaria. He was a prophet of the desert, who controlled, and guided the affairs of his people. To his chagrin, his people worshipped idols and were not willing to listen to him and fear God, the Lord and Cherisher of the world.[1]

So also was Prophet Elias among those sent by us.

Behold he said to his people: "Will ye not fear (Allah)?" "Will ye call upon Baal and forsake the Best of Creators "Allah" your Lord and Cherisher and the Lord and Cherisher of your fathers of old?" However, they rejected him and they will certainly be called up (for punishment) except the sincere and devoted Servants of Allah (among them). And We left (this blessing) for him among generations (to come) in later times: Peace and salutation to such as Elias! Thus indeed do We reward those who do right. For He was one of Our believing Servants.[2]

In the end, the Prophet Elias hoped that his people would believe in God and the afterlife. He tried to convince them that worshipping *Baal* (an ancient idol) would not lead them to peace in the afterlife and that peace and unity would not prevail unless they loved one another and believed that God was their creator. He was determined to duly guide them, but to his exhaustion, they were never able to discover God, the true source of peace.

Chapter 19

Prophet Al-Yasa—*Elisha*

The Prophet Al-Yasa was the cousin and spiritual successor of the Prophet Elias. One day when he saw the Prophet Elias walking through his fields, he dropped his work and followed him. When the Prophet Elias realized that he had left everything to be with him, he questioned him. Prophet Al-Yasa informed him that he wished to accompany him wherever he went. The Prophet Elias consented. In the end, when the Prophet Elias was terminally ill, he asked the Prophet Al-Yasa if he had any desires. The Prophet Al-Yasa indicated that he wished that God would bless him the same way he had blessed the Prophet Elias. His wish was granted and he became one of God's favorites.

The Prophet Al-Yasa is mentioned only twice in the Holy Qur'an:

"And commemorate Isma'il, Elisha and Zul-kifl; each of them was of the company of the good."[1]

"And Zachariah and John and Jesus and Elias all in the ranks of the righteous; and Isma'il and Elisha and Jonah and Lot; each have We preferred above the nations. (To them) and their fathers and progeny and brethren, We chose them and We guided them to a straight way."[2]

Eventually, he traveled to a village where he found its people stricken with starvation. Even though there was no food and the land was barren, the inhabitants still gave him a warm reception. He asked God to grant them bounties, and his prayers were answered.[3]

It is not obvious why some suffer and others not; however, it is quite clear from the examples that God has set forth through His prophets that total submission is the main route to peace. The stories of the prophets reveal that we will rejoice on the day that God reclaims our souls and sifts those of us who believed in Him from those who did not. God has placed us on earth for a reason and we will never find peace until we cease to struggle for worldly treasures. We must submit to God and trust in His plan. He will always respond to the cries of the poor, destitute, and hungry and will gift them with eternal life, a life free of sorrow and desperation. The Prophet Al-Yasa did his best to promote peace, and he was confident that by devoting and submitting one's self to God and believing Him, one may realize the ultimate reward: eternal peace.

Chapter 20

Prophet Yunus—*Jonah*

The Prophet Yunus was instructed through Divine power to educate the people of the Assyrian capital of Nineveh to believe in God. When his first warning was ignored, he declared God's wrath on them. As a result, the Prophet Yunus left his people and was sadly discouraged at the apparent failure of his mission, even though he should have remained and relied on the power of God, who eventually forgave them.

He joined a group of men who were mounting a ship at sea. The ship was overloaded as it faced a heavy storm. The sailors realized that the ship was too heavy and chose to lighten its load by asking one person to jump overboard. To be fair, they decided to cast their votes. The Prophet Yunus's name was first to be picked, but they were hesitant to throw him overboard because they perceived him to be a respectable man, so they tried again. When his name was chosen once more, they had no choice but to demand that he cast himself into the sea.

He was swallowed by a big fish or whale, but in the depth of the darkness, he cried to God, confessed his lack of patience, and repeated several times *La illaha ila Allah* (there is no god, but God). God forgave him and brought him ashore. He sheltered him with a plant that helped to heal his wounds and gave him nourishment. Once he was refreshed and strengthened, he returned to his people and the work of his mission prospered. Thus, he overcame his disappointment by repentance and faith, and God exonerated him. The Prophet Yunus's story invites one not to be impatient but to be forgiving and to allow God's plan to prevail.[1]

> And remember Zun-nun, when he departed in wrath, he imagined that We had no power over him! But he cried through the depths of darkness, "There is no god but Thou; glory to Thee; I was indeed wrong!"[2]

> … Jonah was among those sent (by us). When he ran away (like slave from captivity) to the ship (fully) laden. He (agreed to) cast lots and he was condemned: Then the big Fish did swallow him and he had done acts worthy of blame. Had it not been that he (repented and) glorified Allah. He would certainly have remained inside the Fish until the Day of Resurrection. However, We cast him forth on the naked shore in a state of sickness. And We caused to grow over him a spreading plant of the Gourd kind. And We sent him (on a mission) to a hundred thousand (men) or more. And they believed; so We permitted them to enjoy (their life) for a while.[3]

> Why was there not a single township (among those We warned) who believed so its Faith should have profited it except the people of Jonah? When they believed We removed from them the Penalty of Ignominy in the life of the Present and permitted them to enjoy (their life) for a while. If it had been the Lord's Will they would all have believed all who are on earth! Wilt thou then compel humanity against their will to believe![4]

The Prophet Yunus's story makes it clear that God's prophets are only human, and just as it might be difficult to be patient in the face of those who cling to the status quo and resist believing in God, it is equally difficult to expand one's bosom with patience and believe that only God has the fundamental power to make people change.

The Prophet Yunus despaired when he saw that his people were not going to change or center their minds on God. The story of the Prophet Yunus might have been a test of faith where in the end God showed the prophet that only He has power over life and death. God almost took the Prophet Yunus's life, and yet He gave it back to him when no earthly power could have done so. God wanted the Prophet Yunus to find ways to draw his people closer to Him without walking away in despair. In the end, there cannot be a world of peace in the absence of faith. The Prophet Yunus needed to trust that God would have helped him unify his people in peace if he had understood that *trusting in Him* coincides with believing in Him.

Chapter 21

Prophet Zakariah—*Zachary*

The Prophet Zakariah was a holy person. Both he and his wife were devout and conscientious of their responsibilities toward God. They were old and had no son. The Prophet Zakariah was troubled, not so much by the urge to have a son to carry on his line, but by the selfishness and insincerity of his people. He yearned for a child that he himself could train to worship God.

Eventually, God responded to his prayers and gave him a son, the Prophet Yahya (John the Baptist.) The Prophet Yahya was a fine young man and added to the pious reputation of the family. He was labeled "the noble, the chaste, and the Prophet."[1]

(This is) a recital of the Mercy of thy Lord to His Servant Zakariah.

Behold! He cried to his Lord in secret praying: "O my Lord!" "Infirm indeed are my bones and the hair of my head doth glisten with grey: but never am I unblessed O my Lord in my prayer to Thee!" "Now I fear (what) my relatives (and colleagues) (will do) after me, but my wife is barren" "So give me an heir as from Thyself (One that) will (truly) represent me and represent the posterity of Jacob; and make him O my Lord one with whom Thou art well-pleased!"

(His prayer was answered): O Zakariah! We give thee good news of a son: his name shall be Yahya. On none by that name have We conferred distinction before.

Zakariah said: "O my Lord!" "How shall I have a son when my wife is barren and I have grown quite decrepit from old age?"

Allah revealed: So (it will be): thy Lord saith, That is easy for Me. I did indeed create thee before when thou hadst been nothing!

(Zakariah) said: "O my Lord!" "Give me a Sign."

Allah revealed: Thy Sign is that thou shalt speak to no man for three nights although thou art not dumb.

So Zakariah came out to his people from his chamber. He told them by signs to celebrate Allah's praises in the morning and in the evening.[2] So, We listened to him: and We granted him Yahya: We cured his wife's (barrenness) for him. These three were ever quick in emulation in good works: they used to call on Us with love and reverence and humble themselves before Us.[3]

The Prophet Zakariah was inspired by God to take charge of Mary, the mother of the Prophet Jesus.

Right graciously did her Lord accept her: He made her grow in purity and beauty; she was assigned to the care of Zakariah. Every time that he entered (her) chamber to see her, he found her supplied with sustenance.

He said: "O Mary!" "Whence (comes) this to you?"

She said: "From Allah: for Allah provides sustenance to whom He pleases without measure."[4]

The Prophet Zakariah was a firm believer in God and His power. He prayed to God day and night knowing that God was at the center of man's origin. By secluding himself from the world and surrendering his heart to God, he was able to cleanse his mind from earthly distractions and achieve peace from within. He stepped beyond the boundaries of God's incomprehensible mystery and drew himself and his people toward a land of peace and spiritual happiness.

Chapter 22

Prophet Yahya—*John the Baptist*

The Prophet Yahya was the son of the Prophet Zakariah. The Prophet Zakariah prayed to God to bless him with a son he could train to be a successful heir and preach in the name of God. As mentioned in the previous chapter, God responded to the Prophet Zakariah's prayers and gave him the Prophet Yahya.

The Prophet Yahya lived a simple and humble life. He was the cousin and precursor of the Prophet Issa. He met his fate at the hands of Herod Antipas, the Roman ruler of Galilee.[1]

"O Zakariah!" "We give thee good news of a son: his name shall be Yahya: on none by that name have We conferred distinction before."[2]

(To his son came the command): "O Yahya!" "Take hold of the Book with might": and We gave him wisdom even as a youth."

And pity (for all creatures) as from Us and purity: he was devout and kind to his parents and he was not overbearing or rebellious. So Peace on him the day he was born the day that he dies and the day that he will be raised up to life (again)![3]

God loved His prophets, gifted them with wisdom, and protected them from any harm. He responded to their dreams and supplications and harmonized their souls with peace so that they might, in turn, strengthen their presence in the universe and draw their people closer to them and to God's omnipresence.

Chapter 23

Prophet Issa—*Jesus*

The Prophet Issa's prophecy began from the day he was in the cradle to the age of thirty-three or until his alleged crucifixion as stated in the verse below. His story starts with the birth of his mother Mariam (Mary) and the parallel story the Prophet Yahya, the son of the Prophet Zakariah. The Prophet Yahya's mother Elisabeth was a cousin of Mariam, the mother of the Prophet Issa; therefore the Prophet Yahya and the Prophet Issa were second cousins by blood, and there was a spiritual tie between them throughout their lives.

Even though the life of the Prophet Issa on earth was a call for peace among mankind, it remains a mystery to many before and after what was perceived as his death. Not much is known about his private life, especially during the last three years, when most of his prophecy took place. Cardinal Christians believe that his life was taken on the cross and that he rose from death after the third day of his crucifixion. The Qur'an sheds light on this matter and clarifies that the Prophet Issa was never crucified, even though he may have appeared to be crucified to those who were around him at the time.[1]

Behold! A woman (his wife) of Imran said: "O my Lord!" "I do dedicate unto thee what is in my womb for Thy special service so accept this of me for Thou hearest and knowest all things."

When she was delivered she said: "O my Lord!" "Behold!" "I am delivered of a female child!"

And Allah knew best what she brought forth, and nowise is the male like the female...[2]

In Judaism, the female child could not be devoted to the Temple's service; however, she could be marked out for a special destiny. She was destined to be the mother of the miracle-child Prophet Issa. Her mother bequeathed her to God and sought His protection over her against all evil.[3]

"...I have named her Mary and I commend her and her offspring to Thy protection from the Evil One the Rejected."[4]

Behold! The angels said: "O Mary!" "Allah hath chosen thee and purified thee; chosen thee above the women of all nations." "O Mary!" "Worship thy Lord devoutly; prostrate thyself and bow down (in prayer) with those who bow down."

This is part of the tidings of the things unseen which We reveal unto thee O Apostle! (Prophet Muhammad *(pbuh)*) by inspiration; thou wast not with them when they cast lots with arrows as to which of them should be charged with the care of Mary; nor wast thou with them when they disputed (the point).

Behold the angels said: "O Mary!" "Allah giveth thee glad tidings of a Word from Him: his name will be Christ, Jesus the son of Mary held in honor in this world and the Hereafter and of (the company of) those nearest to Allah." "He shall speak to the people in childhood and in maturity and he shall be (of the company) of the righteous."

Islamic scripture confirms that Mariam, the mother of the Prophet Issa, was special in that she gave birth to him without physical intervention. She was addressed by angels who conveyed God's message to her, and she replied,

> She said: "O my Lord!" "How shall I have a son when no man hath touched me?"

> He said: Even so: Allah createth what He willeth; when He hath decreed a plan He but saith to it 'Be' and it is!

Mariam, the mother of the Prophet Issa, was unique, in that God lifted her above all women and breathed Issa into her womb. Her miraculous pregnancy proved to her that she was taken by a power beyond her control and was destined to submit herself and her son to God.

> "And Allah will teach him the Book and Wisdom the Law and the Gospel." "And (appoint him) an Apostle to the Children of Israel (with this message) …"

> Jesus said: "I (Jesus) have come to you with a sign from your Lord in that I make for you out of clay as it were the figure of a bird and breathe into it and it becomes a bird by Allah's leave; and I heal those born blind and the lepers and I quicken the dead by Allah's leave; and I declare to you what ye eat and what ye store in your houses." "Surely therein is a Sign for you if ye did believe." "(I have come to you) to attest the Law which was before me and to make lawful to you part of what was (before) forbidden to you; I have come to you with a Sign from your Lord. So fear Allah and obey me." "It is Allah who is my Lord and your Lord; then worship Him." "This is a way that is straight."[5]

> When (Jesus) the son of Mary is held as an example, behold thy people raise a clamor thereat (in ridicule)! And they say, "Are our gods best or He?" This, they set forth to thee only by way of

disputation: yea they are a contentious people. He was no more than a servant: We granted Our favor to him and We made him an example to the Children of Israel. And if it were Our Will We could make angels from amongst you succeeding each other on the earth.[6]

God sent the Prophet Issa to be a prophet to the Children of Israel. Those who believed in him became Christian, and those who perceived him as an ordinary man did not. As Christianity began to spread, the pagan Arabs were also among those who did not perceive the Prophet Issa to be any better than their own Gods or idols. However, with the initiation of Islam through the teachings of Prophet Muhammad, the Qur'an reveals that the Prophet Issa was a miracle child and one of God's superior prophets whose mission was to lead his people to believe in God and His Oneness.[7] Muslims believe that the Prophet Issa was one of the five superior messengers of God, the others being the Prophets Nuh, Ibrahim, and Musa, along with Prophet Muhammad *(pbuh.)*

And (Jesus) shall be a Sign (for the coming of) the Hour (of Judgment): therefore have no doubt about the (Hour) but follow ye Me: this is a Straight Way.[8]

This refers to the second coming of the Prophet Issa before the Day of Judgment, when he will destroy the false doctrines that passed under his name. He will pave the way for universal acceptance of Islam as directed by the Qur'an, the Gospel of Unity and Peace.[9]

Let not the Evil One hinder you: for he is to you an enemy avowed.

When Jesus came with Clear Signs he said: "Now have I come to you with Wisdom and in order to make clear to you some of the (points) on which ye dispute: therefore fear Allah and obey me." "For Allah; He is my Lord and your Lord: so worship ye Him: this is a Straight Way."

But sects from among themselves fell into disagreement: then woe to the wrongdoers from the Penalty of a Grievous Day! Do they only wait for the Hour that it should come on them all of a sudden while they perceive not?[10]

And remember Jesus the son of Mary said: "O Children of Israel!" "I am the apostle of Allah (sent) to you confirming the Law (which came) before me and giving glad Tidings of an Apostle to come after me whose name shall be Ahmad." But when he came to them with Clear Signs…

They said: "This is evident sorcery!"[11]

This verse reveals that "Ahmad," or "Muhammad," (a derivative of the same word) the Praised One, was clearly going to ensue after the Prophet Issa.

When Jesus found unbelief on their part he said: "Who will be my helpers to (the work of) Allah?"

Said the Disciples: "We are Allah's helpers. We believe in Allah and do thou bear witness that we are Muslims." "Our Lord!" "We believe in what thou hast revealed and we follow the Apostle; then write us down among those who bear witness."

Moreover, the unbelievers plotted and planned and Allah too planned and the best of planners is Allah.

Behold! Allah revealed: O Jesus! I will take thee and raise thee to Myself and clear thee (of the falsehoods) of those who blaspheme; I will make those who follow thee superior to those who reject Faith to the Day of Resurrection; then shall ye all return unto Me and I will judge between you of the matters wherein ye dispute.[12] This similitude of Jesus before Allah is as that of Prophet Adam:

He created him from dust then said to him: "Be" and he was.[13]

Even though the Prophet Issa occupied a high position in this world, God compared him to the Prophet Adam in that he, too, was born without a human father. The Prophet Issa was a human being, and according to the Qur'an, it is against reason and revelation to call him God or the son of God. He is referred to throughout the Qur'an as the son of Mariam to emphasize this point. He is raised to a high position as a prophet because God called him to his order. The praise is due to God, Who strengthened him with the Holy Spirit. The Qur'an states clearly that those who misunderstood him denied his clear Signs and surrounded him with mysteries of their own invention.[14] They rejected his faith and uttered grave and false charges against his mother Mariam.

The fact that Mariam was accused of being unchaste brought into mockery the power of God. "Islam is especially strong in guarding the reputation of women. Slanderers of women are bound to bring four witnesses in support of their accusations, and if they fail to produce four witnesses, they are to be flogged with eighty stripes and debarred from being competent witnesses."[15]

> That they said (in boast), "We killed Christ Jesus the son of Mary the Apostle of Allah," but they killed him not nor crucified him but so it was made to appear to them and those who differ therein are full of doubts with no (certain) knowledge but only conjecture to follow for of a surety they killed him not. Nay Allah raised him up unto Himself; and Allah is Exalted in Power Wise. And there is none of the People of the Book but must believe in him before his death; and on the Day of Judgment He will be a witness against them.[16]

O people of the Book! Commit no excesses in your religion: nor say of Allah aught but truth. Christ, Jesus the son of Mary was (no more than) an Apostle of Allah and His Word which He bestowed on Mary and a Spirit proceeding from Him: so believe in Allah and His Apostles. Say not "Trinity": desist: it will be better for you: for Allah is One Allah: glory be to him: (for Exalted is He) above having a son. To Him belong all things in the heavens and on earth. And enough is Allah as a Disposer of affairs. Christ disdaineth not to serve and worship Allah nor do the angels those nearest (to Allah): those who disdain His worship and are arrogant He will gather them all together unto himself to (answer).[17]

God is independent of all needs and does not need a son to manage His affairs.[18]

Curses were pronounced on those among the Children of Israel who rejected faith by the tongue of David and of Jesus the son of Mary: because they disobeyed and persisted in excesses.[19]

Behold! The disciples said: "O Jesus the son of Mary!" "Can thy Lord send down to us a table set (with viands) from heaven?"

Jesus said: "Fear Allah if ye have faith."

They said, "We only wish to eat thereof and satisfy our hearts and to know that thou hast indeed told us the truth; and that we ourselves may be witnesses to the miracle."

Jesus said: "O Allah our Lord, send us from heaven a table set (with viands) that there may be for us for the first and the last of us a solemn festival and a sign from Thee; and provide for our sustenance for Thou art the best Sustainer (of our needs)."

Allah revealed: I will send it down unto you: but if any of you after that resisteth faith I will punish him with a penalty such as I have not inflicted on anyone among all the peoples. And behold! Allah will say, O Jesus the son of Mary! Didst thou say unto men 'worship me and my mother as gods in derogation of Allah'? He will say, "Glory to Thee!" "Never could I say what I had no right (to say)." "Had I said such a thing Thou wouldst indeed have known it." "Thou knowest what is in my heart though I know not what is in Thine." "For Thou knowest in full all that is hidden."

"Never said I to them aught except what Thou didst command me to say to wit 'Worship Allah my Lord and your Lord'; and I was a witness over them whilst I dwelt amongst them; when Thou didst take me up thou wast the Watcher over them and Thou art a Witness to all things." "If Thou dost punish them they are Thy servants: if Thou dost forgive them Thou art the Exalted the Wise." Allah will say: "This is a day on which the truthful will profit from their truth: theirs are Gardens with rivers flowing beneath their eternal home: Allah well-pleased with them and they with Allah: that is the great Salvation (the fulfillment of all desires). To Allah doth belong the Dominion of the heavens and the earth and all that is therein and it is He who hath power over all things.[20]

The Prophet Issa acknowledged that he was among the mortals and asked God to forgive the nonbelievers.

O ye who believe! Be ye helpers of Allah as said Jesus the son of Mary to the Disciples: "Who will be my helpers to (the work of) Allah?"

The Disciples said: "We are Allah's helpers!"

Then a portion of the Children of Israel believed and a portion disbelieved, but We gave power to those who believed against their enemies and they became the ones that prevailed.[21] And Mary the daughter of 'Imran who guarded her chastity; and We breathed into her (body) of Our spirit; and she testified to the truth of the words of her Lord and of His Revelations and was one of the devout (Servants).[22] And We made the son of Mary and his mother as a Sign: We gave them both shelter on high ground affording rest and security and furnished with springs.[23]

We gave Musa the Book and followed him up with a succession of Apostles; We gave Jesus the son of Mary clear (Signs) and strengthened him with the holy spirit. Is it that whenever there comes to you an Apostle with what ye yourselves desire not ye are puffed up with pride? Some ye called impostors and others ye slay!²⁴ They say, "Allah hath begotten a son;" Glory be to Him. Nay to Him belongs all that is in the heavens and on earth; everything renders worship to Him.²⁵ Those apostles We endowed with gifts some above others: to one of them Allah spoke; others He raised to degrees (of honor) … If Allah had so willed succeeding generations would not have fought among each other after clear (Signs) had come to them but they (chose) to wrangle some believing, and others rejecting. If Allah had so willed they would not have fought each other; but Allah fulfills His plan.²⁶

God has a plan, and we are all destined to live by it. He sent His prophets so that they might remind us of His presence, and even though many chose to mock, ridicule, or destroy them, they were never able to obliterate God's message, primarily, the belief in God, the One and only. The Prophet Issa spent three years trying to convince his people that God was the underlying power behind his miracles and that the only way to salvation was to believe in His message and unite in peace and harmony. He affirmed that he was God's messenger and that he was fulfilling God's plan and leading them to the Kingdom of Heaven found primarily within their souls. He assured them that the Almighty was the source of worldly peace and eternal happiness, but very few believed him. He was a threat to the status quo and to the supremacy of the ruling powers.

Chapter 24

Prophet Muhammad *(pbuh)*

The Qur'an, the only living document considered the direct word of God, was revealed to the Prophet Muhammad *(pbuh)* in order that he may address all people. Its purpose is to finalize God's word, emphasize the importance of peace, and seal the belief in One God in order to correct any distortions or misinterpretations of previous religions and revelations that took place prior to the birth of Prophet Muhammad *(pbuh)*.

> It is He Who sent down to thee (step by step) in truth the Book confirming what went before it; and He sent down Law (Of Moses) and the Gospel (of Jesus) before this as a guide to mankind and He sent down the Criterion (of judgment between right and wrong.)[1]

Prophet Muhammad *(pbuh)* was born in Mecca, Saudi Arabia in 570 CE. The word Muhammad means "the praised one." He was given his name by his grandfather, Abdul-Muttalib, who believed that his grandson was special and required praise. His mother was Amina, the daughter of Wahab, and his father was Abdallah, the son of Abdul-Muttalib of the Banu Hashim clan of the Quraish tribe, direct descendants of the Prophet Ibrahim and his son, the Prophet Isma'il.

Prophet Muhammad's *(pbuh)* father had gone on a trade caravan trip to Syria, became ill and passed away in Medina or Yathrib, Saudi Arabia before Prophet Muhammad *(pbuh)* was even born. His mother, Amina, died when he was about six years old, leaving him to the care of his grandfather, Abdul-Muttalib, and a governess, namely Halima Al-Saadya. His grandfather's love and care ended a few years later when he passed away, leaving Prophet Muhammad *(pbuh)* under the guidance of Abu Talib, his paternal uncle who had become the new leader of the Hashim clan of the Quraish tribe, the most powerful tribe in Mecca.[2]

Prophet Muhammad *(pbuh)* joined his uncle Abu Talib on a business trip to Damascus, Syria, at around the age of twelve. During his first caravan trip, Abu Talib had made a stop in Busra. Buhayrah, a Nestorian (Christian) monk who watched the caravan, noticed that a cloud was shadowing Prophet Muhammad *(pbuh)* from the heat of the sun. He was suspicious and invited Abu Talib and his company for dinner. During dinner, he carefully observed the young man and knew that, according to some old manuscripts, Prophet Muhammad *(pbuh)* was the predicted prophet. His prediction is also stated in the Qur'an. Note that in Arabic, the words Ahmad and Muhammad are derivatives of the same verb.

> And remember, Jesus, the son of Mary, said: "O Children of Israel! I am the apostle of Allah (sent) to you, confirming the Law (which came) before me, and giving Glad Tidings of a Messenger to come after me, whose name shall be Ahmad." But when he came to them with Clear Signs, they said, "this is evident sorcery!"[3]

Over the years, Prophet Muhammad *(pbuh)* was found to be a fine, trusting young man. When his uncle Abu Talib became old and financially weak, he advised Prophet Muhammad *(pbuh)* to work for Khadija bint Khuwaylid, twice a widow and among the wealthiest of the Quraish. She had heard of Prophet Muhammad's *(pbuh)* reputation as an honest man and asked him to sell goods for her in Syria. He agreed. When he returned and she realized that he was very successful, she sent him again. Even though she had received many suitors, upon Prophet Muhammad's *(pbuh)* second return, she was convinced that she had finally found the man she could trust and with whom she could spend the rest of her life. Although she was approximately fifteen years his senior, they joined each other in matrimony in 595 CE.[4]

Prophet Muhammad *(pbuh)* was born into Arabia's Jahiliya (age of ignorance) and spent most of his middle-age years retreating to the cave of Hira to meditate and reflect on the world around him. He was perplexed by the beliefs of those who did not believe in God and who believed that life was a natural occurrence, until he was visited by the Archangel Jibril;

> And they say: "What is there but our life in this world?" "We shall die and we live and nothing but Time can destroy us." But of that they have no knowledge: they merely conjecture.[5]

It is at the age of forty that the Archangel Jibril first visited him. The angel directed Prophet Muhammad to recite the sura (the chapter) of al-Alaq:

> "Proclaim! in the name of thy Lord and Cherisher Who created. Created man out of a (mere) cLut of congealed blood: Proclaim! And thy Lord is Most Bountiful."

> He Who taught (the use of) the Pen; Taught man that which he knew not. Nay but man doth transgress all bounds in that he looketh upon himself as self-sufficient. Verily to thy Lord is the return (of all). Seest thou one who forbids. A votary when he (turns) to pray? Seest thou if He is on (the road of) Guidance? Or enjoins Righteousness? Seest thou if he denies (Truth) and turns away? Knoweth he not that Allah doth see? Let him beware! If he desist not We will drag him by the forelock. A lying sinful forelock! Then let him call (for help) to his council (of comrades): We will call on the angels of punishment (to deal with him)! Nay heed him not: but bow down in adoration and bring thyself the closer (to Allah)![6]

Note that he word "Iqra" means "read". However, Prophet Muhammad was illiterate; hence "Iqra" can be assumed to mean proclaim.

Shaken and terrified by the power and weight of his mission, Prophet Muhammad *(pbuh)* shared his experience with his wife Khadija. She believed his account and encouraged him to believe that he was indeed God's chosen prophet and was chosen to lift the Arabs from the age of Jahiliya.

The Prophet *(pbuh)* cautiously began his mission but was met with the strong opposition of Abu Sufian and his paternal uncle Abu Lahab who believed he was bewitched. They were in control of the Kabaa, that had over the years been converted to the sanctuary of the Meccans, as well as the hundreds of idols that marked their political and economic control over Mecca. To keep Prophet Muhammad *(pbuh)* safe and protect him from the wrath of his evil brother, Abu Talib warned the Prophet *(pbuh)* to sleep in a different place at all times. Abu Jahl, one of the Prophet's foes, had set a reward of one hundred camels or one thousand ounces of gold for whoever might kill him. In search of the award, Omar Bin Khattab set out to kill him. Upon entering Prophet Muhammad's *(pbuh)* doorsteps, he encountered Prophet Muhammad's *(pbuh)* uncle Hamzah who had chosen to embrace Islam. Hamzah invited him in to see the Prophet *(pbuh)* and Omar instantly began to tremble as he stood before him and looked intently at his face. The Prophet *(pbuh)*, cognizant of Omar's prior motive, welcomed him to Islam.[7]

Abu Talib remained Prophet Muhammad's *(pbuh)* shield and guardian against his own tribe, the Quraish. They tried to negotiate the trade of Prophet Muhammad *(pbuh)* for another wise young man, but Abu Talib adamantly refused. From the Quraish perspective, Prophet Muhammad *(pbuh)* was a threat to their polytheistic faith and power. As a result, in the year 616 CE the Quraish and all tribes who opposed Prophet Muhammad's *(pbuh)* popularity decided to sever their ties with the entire clans of Hashim and Muttalib, socially and economically. This was their way of forcing them to starve and possibly stop the growth of Islam. The document was signed by Prophet Muhammad's *(pbuh)* enemies and hung in the Kabaa. The estrangment lasted for three long years, and it exhausted Prophet Muhammad *(pbuh)* and his Ummah (the followers of Islam). In addition, to Prophet Muhammad's *(pbuh)* chagrin, he lost his wife and confidant Khadija and his uncle and protector, Abu Talib, shortly after the boycott had ended, leaving him subject to the verbal assaults and abuse of his enemies.[8]

His uncle Abu Lahab openly declared his hatred of Prophet Muhammad *(pbuh)* and refused to protect him from the abuse he encountered in the streets of Mecca. At this point, Prophet Muhammad *(pbuh)* had no choice but to emigrate. He sent seventy of his followers ahead of him to the city of Yathrib some 250 miles away. The emigration was done gradually to eliminate suspicion. Prophet Muhammad *(pbuh)*, his cousin Ali (Abu Talib's son), and his companion Abu Bakr were among the last to leave. Prophet Muhammad *(pbuh)* had learned of that the Quraish had plotted to kill him. Fortunately, Prophet Muhammad *(pbuh)* did not sleep in his bed that night, and the enemies were deceived when they found that his cousin Ali had slept in his place. Angered, the Quraish announced a massive reward for Prophet Muhammad's *(pbuh)* death. Prophet Muhammad *(pbuh)* along with Abu Bakr fled and took cover in a cave near Mecca.[9] Abu Bakr was afraid, but Prophet Muhammad *(pbuh)* encouraged him not to worry and reassured him that God would protect them.

> If ye help not (your Leader) (it is no matter) for Allah did indeed help him. When the unbelievers drove him out, he had no more than one companion. They two were in the cave and he said to his companion, "Have no fear for Allah is with us."

> Then Allah sent down his peace upon him and strengthened him with forces which ye saw not and humbled to the depths the word of the unbelievers. But the word of Allah is exalted to the heights: for Allah is Exalted in might Wise.[10]

As soon as Prophet Muhammad *(pbuh)* entered the cave, a spider miraculously wove a web, and a pair of pigeons built their nest at its entrance. This helped to divert his enemies away from the cave. Prophet Muhammad *(pbuh)*, then fifty-three years of age, entered Yathrib, known today as Medina (the city of the prophet) and laid the foundations of the first mosque, namely Quba Mosque, also referred to as Masjid al-Taqwa (the mosque of piety.) Thus, the year 622 CE became known as the first calendar year of Islam, the year of Hijra or Emigration.

During the age of Jahiliya, the only way to become a member of a tribe was to be born into it where this was not so in Islam. By submitting one's will to God and uttering the words "la illaha ila Allah wa Muhammad *(pbuh)* rasoul Allah" (there is no God but God, and Prophet Muhammad *(pbuh)* is God's messenger), one became a member of the Ummah. Also, the fact that the prophet had married nine women (mostly widowed) to help protect them and their children and safeguard their dignity was a sign of care and devotion, not lust and desire. He had hoped to set the example for other Muslims to follow and provide protection to widows and their orphaned children.[11] Even though God inspired Prophet Muhammad (*pbuh*) to marry nine women, He cautions all other men not to marry more than four. If for any reason a man chooses to marry more than one wife, he must treat his wives equally in every respect, which God claims may be difficult or impossible.

> If ye fear that ye shall not be able to deal justly with the orphans marry women of your choice two or three or four; but if ye fear that ye shall not be able to deal justly (with them) then only one or (a captive) that your right hands possess. That will be more suitable to prevent you from doing injustice.[12] Ye are never able to be fair and just as between women even if it is your ardent desire: but turn not away (from a woman) altogether so as to leave her (as it were) hanging (in the air). If ye come to a friendly understanding and practice self-restraint Allah is Oft-Forgiving Most Merciful.[13]

The news that Islam was growing in Medina infuriated the Quraish, and they began to make preparations to kill him. To do so, they gathered a large army and marched toward Medina in 624 CE. Prophet Muhammad *(pbuh)* was prepared, and he defeated the Quraish at what is known historically as the Battle of Badr. A year later, the Quraish prepared to avenge Prophet Muhammad *(pbuh)* and attacked him and his followers at the Battle of Uhud. After the battle, the Jews and the Quraish were frightened and vowed to fight Prophet Muhammad *(pbuh)* for as long as they lived. Once again, Prophet Muhammad *(pbuh)* and his followers faced and defeated their enemies at the Battle of Khandaq (trench) in 627 CE and the Battle of Khaybar (fortified city) in 628 CE.[14]

Shortly after the defeat, Prophet Muhammad *(pbuh)* signed a peace treaty (Treaty of Hudaybiyya) for a cease-fire with the Meccans and, accompanied by two thousand Muslims, visited Mecca for a few days. This was Prophet Muhammad's *(pbuh)* way to build the trust of the people. A year later, he conquered Mecca after the Meccans had breached the treaty. The Meccans surrendered, with the exception of Abu Soufian, who still had doubts about his prophethood and chose not to greet him. Prophet Muhammad *(pbuh)* then made his way to the Kabaa and broke over three hundred and sixty idols fixed to its walls claiming:

"Truth has now arrived, and falsehood perished: for falsehood is by nature, bound to perish."[15]

By 630 CE Islam was accepted by multitudes of Meccans and their surrounding tribes, and by then, pagans were forbidden from entering the Kabaa.

In 632 CE Prophet Muhammad *(pbuh)* performed his last pilgrimage in Mecca, returned to Medina, and passed away at the age of sixty-three. His death devastated the believers, who thought that it was inconceivable for the messenger of God to die. However, his supporters claimed, "O men, if anyone worships Prophet Muhammad *(pbuh)*, Prophet Muhammad *(pbuh)* is dead; if anyone worships God, God is alive, immortal!"[16]

According to the Qur'an, the word Muslim, as mentioned earlier, means "one whose will is submitted to God." Thus, those who believe that there is Only one God and that Prophet Muhammad *(pbuh)* is His final messenger are Muslims in faith. God welcomes and protects all those who join Islam. However, Muslims who change their faith and follow a religion other than Islam will find no protection from God.

"If ye backslide after the clear (Signs) have come to you, then know that Allah is Exalted in Power, Wise."[17]

In addition, God challenges those who claim that only Jews and Christians shall enter paradise to produce a proof of that claim, and

He maintains that everyone must carefully study the Qur'an in order to bring clarity to this matter.

> Some have said, "No one will enter Paradise except Jews or Christians!" Such is their wishful thinking. Say, "Show us your proof, if you are right."[18]

The majority of verses below are among many in the Qur'an where God instructed Prophet Muhammad *(pbuh)* to respond to the nonbelievers:

> "We believe in Allah and the revelation given to us and to Abraham, Isma'il, Isaac, Jacob, and the Tribes and that given to Musa and Jesus and that given to (all) Prophets from their Lord." "We make no difference between one or the other and we bow to Allah (in Islam)."[19]

If they choose to accept Islam as a religion, He is most merciful and most forgiving. God listens to every prayer when called upon and warns that we must listen to His call and believe in Him and choose the right path. Prophet Muhammad *(pbuh)* is verily an apostle of God, and it is his mission to spread the word but not to coerce people into believing in Islam, since God is the final judge of all. The Prophet *(pbuh)* will witness over those who believed and those who did not, and God will guide those who turn their faces to the heavens and ask Him for guidance. God sent the Book in truth and affirms that it should not be disputed. Muslims must turn to God and say:

> "... We hear and we obey; we seek Thy forgiveness our Lord and to Thee is the end of all journeys."[20] "It is Allah Who sent the Qur'an step by step," "... confirming what went before it; and He sent down Law (Of Musa) and the Gospel (of Jesus) before this as a guide to mankind and He sent down the Criterion (of judgment between right and wrong)."[21]

> He it is Who has sent down to thee the Book: in it are verses basic or fundamental of established meaning; they are the foundation of the Book: others are allegorical. But those in whose hearts is

perversity follow the part thereof that is allegorical seeking discord and searching for its hidden meanings, but no one knows its hidden meanings except Allah and those who are firmly grounded in knowledge say: "We believe in the Book; the whole of it is from our Lord; and none will grasp the Message except men of understanding."[22]

For those who question the Qur'an, God has sent signs for them:

Ye People of the Book! Why reject ye the Signs of Allah of which ye are (yourselves) witnesses?[23] Ye People of the Book! Why do ye clothe truth with falsehood and conceal the truth while ye have knowledge?[24] We have sent to you (O men!) an apostle to be a witness concerning you even as We sent an apostle to Pharaoh.[25] "Nay, they say, "(these are) medleys of dreams!" "Nay he forged it!" "…Nay he is (but) a poet!" "Let him then bring us a Sign like the ones that were sent to (prophets) of old!"[26]

It is not (possible) that a man to whom is given the Book and Wisdom and the prophetic office should say to people: "Be ye my worshippers rather than Allah's." On the contrary (he would say), "Be ye worshippers of Him Who is truly the Cherisher of all for ye have taught the Book and ye have studied it earnestly."[27] Muhammad is no more than an Apostle: many were the Apostles that passed away before him. If he died or were slain will ye then turn back on your heels? If any did turn back on his heels not the least harm will he do to Allah; but Allah (on the other hand) will swiftly reward those who (serve him) with gratitude.[28] No prophet could (ever) be false to his trust. If any person is so false He shall on the Day of Judgment restore what he misappropriated; then shall every soul receive its due whatever it earned and none shall be dealt with unjustly.[29]

Thus, every person will be held accountable on the Day of Judgment for his or her deeds. It is out of God's love and care for his people that He sent prophets to remind them of the afterlife and to follow His Scriptures.

Allah did confer a great favor on the believers when He sent among them an Apostle from among themselves rehearsing unto them the Signs of Allah sanctifying them and instructing them in Scripture and Wisdom while before that they had been in manifest error.[30] We send the Apostles only to give good news and to warn: so those who believe and mend (their lives) upon them shall be no fear nor shall they grieve.[31] It is a matter of wonderment to men that We have set Our inspiration to a man from among themselves. That he should warn mankind (of their danger) and give the good news to the Believers that they have before their Lord the lofty rank of Truth (but) say the Unbelievers, "This is indeed an evident sorcerer!"[32]

Unfortunately, the unbelievers mocked and ignored God's warnings and accused Prophet Muhammad *(pbuh)* of forgery.

This Qur'an is not such as can be produced by other than Allah; on the contrary it is a confirmation of (revelations) that went before it and a fuller explanation of the Book wherein there is no doubt from the Lord of the Worlds.[33]

If they charge thee with falsehood say: "My work to me and yours to you!" "Ye are free from responsibility for what I do and I for what ye do!"[34]

Nonetheless, it is Prophet Muhammad's *(pbuh)* duty to inform people that he and his followers have submitted their wills to God and that the Qur'an, is merely the completing chapter of the Old and New Testaments.

In order to help the Prophet *(pbuh)* and his followers strengthen their faith in the Almighty, Prophet Muhammad *(pbuh)* was spiritually and/or literally transported from the Sacred Mosques of Mecca to the farthest Mosque of Jerusalem—the Temple of the Prophet Suleiman on the hill of Moriah at or near the Dome of the Rock in Jerusalem—in a night and shown signs of the Divine. Prophet Muhammad *(pbuh)* was first transported to Jerusalem and then taken to the seven Heavens.

"It is He Who hath created for you all things that are on earth; Moreover His design comprehended the heavens, for He gave order and perfection to the seven firmaments; and of all things He hath perfect knowledge."[35]

The Ascension of Prophet Muhammad *(pbuh)* is usually dated to the night of the twenty-seventh of Rajab in the year before the Hijra.

Glory to (Allah) Who did take His Servant for Journey by night from the Sacred Mosque to the Farthest Mosque whose precincts We did Bless in order that We might show him some of Our Signs: for He is the one Who heareth and seeth (all things).[36]

God helped to minimize people's doubt of the ascension by introducing more details of its occurrence.

Your Companion is neither astray nor being misled Nor does he say (aught) of (his own) Desire. It is no less than inspiration sent down to him: he was taught by one mighty in Power Endued with Wisdom: For he appeared (in stately form) While he was in the highest part of the horizon: Then he approached and came closer And was at a distance of but two bow-lengths or (even) nearer; So did (Allah) convey the inspiration to His Servant (conveyed) what He (meant) to convey. The (Prophet in his mind and heart) did not falsify that which he saw. Will ye then dispute with him concerning what he saw? For indeed he saw him at a second descent. Near the Lute-tree beyond which none may pass: Near it is the Garden of Abode. Behold the Lute-tree was shrouded (in mystery unspeakable!) (His) sight never swerved nor did it go wrong![37]

Prophet Muhammad *(pbuh)* was not going astray, nor did he lack intelligence as alleged by the unbelievers. His revelations revealed beauty, power, and wisdom, and they were undoubtedly a direct inspiration from God.

In the end, those who adopt Islam and practice it faithfully will be rewarded for their deeds on the Day of Judgment. Nonbelievers who consider Islam an imitation or replication of prior religions will never be rewarded or capable of understanding God's message.

> Verily this Qur'an doth guide to that which is most right (or stable) and giveth the glad tidings to the Believers who work deeds of righteousness that they shall have a magnificent reward;[38] When thou dost recite the Qur'an We put between thee and those who believe not in the Hereafter a veil invisible: And We put coverings over their hearts (and minds) lest they should understand the Qur'an and deafness into their ears: when thou dost commemorate thy Lord and Him alone in the Qur'an they turn on their backs fleeing (from the Truth).[39]

God sent His prophets to warn man to call upon Him with sincere devotion and will extend His wrath upon those who mock Prophet Muhammad *(pbuh)* and His commands.

> We have put forth for men in this Qur'an every kind of Parable in order that they may receive admonition.[40] Call ye then upon Allah with sincere devotion to Him even though the Unbelievers may detest it. Raised high above ranks (or degrees) (He is) the Lord of the Throne (of authority): by his command doth He send the spirit (of inspiration) to any of His servants He pleases that it may warn (men) of the Day of Mutual Meeting.[41] We will without doubt help Our apostles and those who believe (both) in this world's life and on the Day when the Witnesses will stand forth. It will be the Day when it will be of no profit to the Wrongdoers to present their excuses, but they will (only) have the Curse and the Home of Misery.[42]

> Muhammad *(pbuh)* is the Apostle of Allah; and those who are with him are strong against Unbelievers (but) compassionate amongst each other. Thou wilt see them bow and prostrate themselves (in prayer) seeking Grace from Allah and (His) Good Pleasure. On their faces are their marks (being) the traces of their prostration. This is their similitude in the Torah; and their similitude in the Gospel is: like a seed which sends forth its blade then makes it strong; it then becomes thick and it stands on its own stem (filling) the sown seeds with wonder and delight. As a result, it fills the

Unbelievers with rage at him. Allah has promised those among them who believe and do righteous deeds Forgiveness and a great Reward.[43]

The Holy Prophet *(pbuh)* taught and embraced Muslims from all over the world, and to his satisfaction, Islam grew and took a life of its own.

All who obey Allah and the Apostle are in the company of those on whom is the Grace of Allah of the Prophets (who teach) the sincere (lovers of truth) the witnesses (who testify) and the righteous (who do good). Ah! What a beautiful fellowship![44] But Allah beareth witness that what He hath sent unto thee He hath sent from His (Own) Knowledge and the angels bear witness: but enough is Allah for a Witness.[45]

God is witness to all that has occurred and everything that is yet to come, and He advises the Prophet *(pbuh)* to stand firm and tells him how to respond to negativity through verses such as those selected below:

If anyone disputes in this matter with thee now after (full) knowledge hath come to thee say: Come! Let us gather together our sons and your sons our women and your women ourselves and yourselves: then let us earnestly pray and invoke the curse of Allah on those who lie![46]

Say: "O people of the Book!" "Come to common terms as between us and you: that we worship none but Allah; that we associate no partners with Him; that we erect not from among ourselves Lords and patrons other than Allah."

If then they turn back say: "Bear witness that we (at least) are Muslims (bowing to Allah's will)."[47]

And if non-Muslims say to one another: "And believe no one

unless he follows your religion."

Say: "True guidance is the guidance of Allah; (fear ye) lest a revelation be sent to someone (else) like unto that which was sent unto you." "Or that those (receiving such revelation) should engage you in argument before your Lord."

Say: "All bounties are in the hand of Allah: He granteth them to whom He pleaseth; and Allah careth for all and He knoweth all things."[48]

Behold! Allah took the covenant of the Prophets saying: I give you a Book and Wisdom; then comes to you an Apostle confirming what is with you; do ye believe him and render him help.

Allah revealed: Do ye agree and take this My Covenant as binding on you?

They said: "We agree."

He said: "Then bear witness and I am with you among the witnesses."[49]

Say: "We believe in Allah and in what has been revealed to us and what was revealed to Abraham, Isma'il, Isaac, Jacob, and the Tribes and in (Books) given to Musa Jesus and the Prophets from their Lord; we make no distinction between one and another among them and to Allah do we bow our will (in Islam)."[50]

They (also) said: "Allah took our promise not to believe in an Apostle unless He showed us a sacrifice consumed by fire (from heaven).”

Say: “There came to you Apostles before me with clear signs and even with what ye ask for: why then did ye slay them if ye speak the truth?”[51]

Say: “Shall I take for my protector any other than Allah the Maker of the heavens and the earth?” “It is He that feeds, but is not fed.”

Say: “Nay!” “But I am commanded to be the first of those who bow to Allah (in Islam) and be not thou of the company of those who join gods with Allah.”

Say: “I would if I disobeyed my Lord indeed have fear of the penalty of a Mighty Day.”[52]

Say: “What thing is most weighty in evidence?”

Say: “Allah is Witness between me and you: this Qur’an hath been revealed to me by inspiration that I may warn you and all whom it reaches.”

And if they say: “Can ye possibly bear witness that besides Allah there is another Allah?”

Say: “Nay!” “I cannot bear witness!”

Say: “But in truth He is the One Allah and I truly am innocent of (your blasphemy of) joining others with Him.”[53]

Say: "I tell you not that with me are the treasures of Allah nor do I know what is hidden nor do I tell you I am an angel." "I but follow what is revealed to me."

Say: "Can the blind be held equal to the seeing?" "Will ye then consider not?"[54]

Say: "Verily my Lord hath guided me to a way that is straight a religion of right the path (trod) by Abraham the true in faith and he (certainly) joined not gods with Allah."[55]

Say: "O men!" "I am sent unto you all as the apostle of Allah to Whom belongeth the Dominion of the heavens and the earth: there is no Allah but He: it is He that giveth both life and death." "So believe in Allah and His apostle the unlettered Prophet who believed in Allah and His words: follow him that (so) ye may be guided."[56]

[And if] They ask thee about the (final) hour when will be its appointed time;

Say: "The knowledge thereof is with my Lord (alone): none but He can reveal as to when it will occur." "Heavy were its burden through the heavens and the earth." "Only all of a sudden will it come to you."

[And if] They ask thee as if thou wert eager in search thereof:

Say: "The knowledge thereof is with Allah (alone) but most men know not."

Say: "I have no power over any good or harm to myself except as Allah willeth." "If I had knowledge of the unseen I should have multiplied all good and no evil should have touched me." "I am but a cautioner and a bringer of glad tidings to those who have faith."[57]

Or do they say: "He forged it?"

Say: "Bring then a Surah like unto it and call (to your aid) anyone you can besides Allah if it be ye speak the truth!"[58]

Say: "If the whole of mankind and Jinns were to gather together to produce the like of this Qur'an they could not produce the like thereof even if they backed up each other with help and support."[59]

Say: "I have no power over any harm or profit to myself except as Allah willeth." "To every People is a term appointed: when their term is reached not an hour can they cause delay nor (an hour) can they advance (it in anticipation)."[60]

Say: "O ye men!" "If ye are in doubt as to my religion (behold!)" "I worship not what ye worship other than Allah, but I worship Allah Who will take your souls (at death): I am commanded to be (in the ranks) of the Believers."[61]

Say: "O ye men!" "Now Truth hath reached you from your Lord!" "Those who receive guidance do so for the good of their own souls; those who stray do so to their own loss: and I am not (set) over you to arrange your affairs."[62]

Say: "If there were settled on earth angels walking about in peace and quiet We should certainly have sent them down from the heavens an angel for an apostle."

Say: "Enough is Allah for a witness between me and you: for He is well-acquainted with His servants and He sees (all things)."[63]

Say: "Whether ye believe in it or not it is true that those who were given knowledge beforehand when it is recited to them fall down on their faces in humble prostration."

Say: "Glory to our Lord!" "Truly has the promise of our Lord been fulfilled!" They fall down on their faces in tears and it increases their (earnest) humility.[64]

Say: "If the ocean were ink (wherewith to write out) the words of my Lord sooner would the ocean be exhausted than would the words of my Lord even if we added another ocean like it for its aid."

Say: "I am but a man like yourselves (but) the inspiration has come to me that your Allah is one Allah: whoever expects to meet his Lord let him work righteousness and in the worship of his Lord admit no one as partner."[65]

Say: "I am no bringer of new-fangled doctrine among the apostles nor do I know what will be done with me or with you." "I follow but that which is revealed to me by inspiration: I am but a Warner open and clear."

Say: "See ye?" "If (this teaching) be from Allah and ye reject it and a witness from among the Children of Israel testifies to its similarity (with earlier scriptures) and has believed while ye are arrogant (how unjust ye are!) Truly Allah guides not a people unjust."[66]

Say: "No reward do I ask of you for this (Qur'an) nor am I a pretender." "This is no less than a Message to (all) the Worlds." "And ye shall certainly know the truth of it (all) after a while."[67]

Say thou: "Await ye!" "I too will wait along with you!"[68]

A section of the People of the Book say: Believe in the morning what is revealed to the believers but reject it at the end of the day; perchance they may (themselves) turn back.[69] Without doubt among men the nearest of kin to Abraham are those who follow him as are also this Apostle and those who believe; and Allah is the Protector of those who have faith. It is the wish of a section of the People of the Book to lead you astray, but they shall lead astray (not you) but themselves and they do not perceive![70] There is among them a section who distort the Book with their tongues; (as they read) you would think it is a part of the Book but it is no part of the Book; and they say, That is from Allah, but it is not from Allah: it is they who tell a lie against Allah and (well) they know it![71] Then, if they reject thee so were rejected Apostles before thee who came with clear Signs Books of dark prophecies and the Book of enlightenment.[72]

We have sent down to thee the Book in truth that thou mightest judge between men as guided by Allah: so be not (used) as an advocate by those who betray their trust.[73] But for the Grace of Allah to thee and His Mercy a party of them would certainly have plotted to lead thee astray. But (in fact) they will only lead their own souls astray and to thee they can do no harm in the least. For Allah hath sent down to thee the Book and wisdom and taught thee what thou knewest not (before); and great is the grace of Allah unto thee.[74]

If We had sent unto thee a written (Message) on parchment so that they could touch it with their hands the unbelievers would have been sure to say: This is nothing but obvious magic! They say, Why is not an angel sent down to him? If We did send down an angel the matter would be settled at once and no respite would be granted them. If We had made it an angel, We should have sent him as a man and We should certainly have caused them confusion in a matter which they have already covered with confusion. Mocked were (many) Apostles before thee, but the scoffers were hemmed in by the thing that they mocked.[75] Lest ye should say: The Book was sent down to two peoples before us and for our part we remained unacquainted with all that they learned by assiduous study. Or lest ye should say, If the Book had only been sent down to us we should have followed its guidance better than they. Now then hath come unto you a Clear (sign) from your Lord and a guide and a mercy: then who could do more wrong than one who rejecteth Allah's signs and turneth away there from? In good time shall We requite those who turn away from Our Signs with a dreadful penalty for their turning away. Are they waiting to see if the angels come to them or thy Lord (Himself) or certain of the signs of thy Lord! The day that certain of the signs of thy Lord do come no good will it do to a soul to believe in them then if it believed not before nor earned righteousness through its Faith.

Say: "Wait ye: we too are waiting."[76]

A Book revealed unto thee so let thy heart be oppressed no more by any difficulty on that account that with it thou mightest warn (the erring) and teach the believers.[77]

God addressed Prophet Muhammad *(pbuh)* by stating the following:

In whatever business thou mayest be and whatever portion thou mayest be reciting from the Qur'an and whatever deed ye (humankind) may be doing We are Witnesses thereof when ye are deeply engrossed therein. Nor is it hidden from thy Lord (so much as) the weight of an atom on the earth or in heaven is hidden. And not the least and not the greatest of these things but are recorded in a clear Record.[78] If thou wert in doubt as to what We have revealed unto thee then ask those who have been reading the Book from before thee: the Truth hath indeed come to thee from thy Lord: so be in nowise of those in doubt.[79] Follow thou the inspiration sent unto thee and be patient and constant till Allah doth decide: for He is the Best to decide.[80]

Perchance thou mayest (feel the inclination) to give up a part of what is revealed unto thee and thy heart feeleth straitened lest they say, "Why is not a treasure sent down unto him or why does not an angel come down with him?"

But thou art there only to warn! It is Allah that arrangeth all affairs! Or they may say "He forged it." Say, "Bring ye then ten Surahs forged like unto it and call (to your aid) whomsoever ye can other than Allah if ye speak the truth!" "If then they (your false gods) answer not your (call) know ye that this Revelation is sent down (replete) with the knowledge of Allah and that there is no Allah but He!" "Will ye even then submit (to Islam)?"[81]

Can they be (like) those who accept a Clear (Sign) from their Lord and whom a witness from Himself doth teach as did the Book of Musa before it a guide and a mercy? They believe therein; but those of the Sects that reject it the Fire will be their promised meeting place. Be not then in doubt thereon: for it is the Truth from thy Lord: yet many among men do not believe![82]

We have sent it down as an Arabic Qur'an in order that ye may learn wisdom. We do relate unto thee the most beautiful of stories in that We reveal to thee this (portion of the) Qur'an: before this thou too wast among those who knew it not.[83] We sent not an apostle except (to teach) in the language of his (own) people in order to make (things) clear to them. Now Allah leaves straying those whom He pleases and guides whom He pleases: and He is Exalted in power Full of Wisdom.[84]

And We sent down the Book to thee for the express purpose that thou shouldst make clear to them those things in which they differ and that it should be a guide and a mercy to those who believe.[85] We know indeed that they say, "It is a man that teaches him." The tongue of him they wickedly point to is notable foreign while this is Arabic pure and clear.[86]

We send down (stage by stage) in the Qur'an that which is a healing and a mercy to those who believe: to the unjust it causes nothing but loss after loss.[87] They say, "We shall not believe in thee until thou cause spring to gush forth for us from the earth; or (until) thou have a garden of date trees and vines and cause rivers to gush forth in their midst carrying abundant water; or thou cause the sky to fall in pieces as thou sayest (will happen) against us; or thou bring Allah and the angels before (us) face to face."[88]

What kept men back from Belief when Guidance came to them was nothing but this: they said, "Has Allah sent a man (like us) to be (His) Apostle?"[89]

We sent down the (Qur'an) in Truth and in Truth has it descended: and We sent thee but to give Glad Tidings and to warn (sinners). (It is) a Qur'an which We have divided (into parts from time to time) in order that thou mightest recite it to men at intervals: We have revealed it by stages.[90]

We have explained in detail in this Qur'an for the benefit of mankind every kind of similitude: but man is in most things contentious.[91] So have We made the (Qur'an) easy in thine own tongue that with it thou mayest give Glad Tidings to the righteous and warnings to people given to contention.[92]

We have not sent down the Qur'an to thee to be (an occasion) for thy distress. But only as an admonition to those who fear Allah.[93] Thus have we sent this down an Arabic Qur'an and explained therein in detail some of the warnings in order that they may fear Allah or that it may cause their remembrance (of Him).[94]

(It is) a Qur'an in Arabic without any crookedness (therein): in order that they may guard against Evil.[95] The Unbelievers say of those who believe: "If (this Message) were a good thing (such men) would not have gone to it first before us!" And seeing that

180

they guide not themselves thereby they will say, "This is an old falsehood!"[96]

Therefore, proclaim thou the praises (of thy Lord): For by the Grace of thy Lord thou art no (vulgar) soothsayer nor art thou one possessed. Or do they say "A Poet!" We await for him some calamity (hatched) by Time![97] Is it that their faculties of understanding urge them to this or are they but a people transgressing beyond bounds? Or do they say, "He fabricated the (Message)?" Nay they have no faith! Let them then produce a recital like unto it if (it be) they speak the Truth! Were they created of nothing or were they themselves the creators? Or did they create the heavens and the earth? Nay they have no firm belief. Or are the Treasures of thy Lord with them or are they the managers (of affairs)? Or have they a ladder by which they can (climb up to heaven and) listen (to its secrets)? Then let (such a) listener of theirs produce a manifest proof. Or has He only daughters and ye have sons? Or is it that thou dost ask for a reward so that they are burdened with a load of debt? Or that the Unseen is in their hands and they write it down?[98]

*   *   *

God created the Prophet Adam and Eve and gave them free will. He instructed them to eat and drink from His bounties and not to yield to the sinful temptations of the devil. Unfortunately, they failed to remember God's command and fell to earth from the Heavenly Garden of Eden. From then onward, man has been through hardship and sin.

Despite man's insubordination, God sent prophets and angels to remind people of His existence and to help prepare them for the Day of Judgment. God did not want man to take "… angels and prophets for Lords and Patrons …" but to listen to their message and to surrender their will to God.[99] Even though commentators disagree on the number of prophets sent by God to reveal His message, there is a consensus that not all of them are mentioned in the Qur'an:

Then after him We sent (Many) apostles to their Peoples: They brought them clear signs, but, they would not believe what they had already rejected beforehand. Thus do We seal the hearts of the transgressors.[100]

And Zakariah and John and Jesus and Elias: all in the ranks of the righteous: And Isma'il and Elisha and Jonas and Lot: and to all We gave favor above the nations: (To them) and to their fathers and progeny and brethren: We chose them. And We guided them to a straight way. This is the guidance of Allah: He giveth that guidance to whom He pleaseth of His worshippers. If they were to join other gods with Him all that they did would be vain for them. These were the men to whom We gave the Book and authority and prophethood: if these (their descendants) reject them behold! We shall entrust their charge to a new People who reject them not. Those were the (Prophets) who received Allah's guidance: copy the guidance they received;

Say: "No reward for this do I ask of you: this is no less than a Message for the nations."[101]

Behold! Allah took the covenant of the prophets, saying: "I give you a Book and Wisdom; then comes to you an apostle, confirming what is with you; do ye believe in him and render him help."

Allah said: "Do ye agree, and take this my Covenant as binding on you?" They said: "We agree." He said: "Then bear witness, and I am with you among the witnesses." If any turn back after this, they are perverted transgressors.

Allah said: Do they seek for other than the Religion of Allah while all creatures in the heavens and on earth have, willing or unwilling, bowed to His Will (Accepted Islam), and to Him shall they all be brought back.

Say: "We believe in Allah, and in what has been revealed to us and what was revealed to Abraham, Isma'il, Isaac, Jacob, and the Tribes, and in (the Books) given to Musa, Jesus, and the prophets, from their Lord: We make no distinction between one and another among them, and to Allah do we bow our will (in Islam)." "[102]

In the end, those who bow to God's will and believe in Him and in the Day of Judgment will certainly find His grace. Not only did God send messengers to help man repent and surrender to His will, but He also created miracles to help reduce all doubt and increase conviction.

Mankind was one single nation and Allah sent Messengers with glad tidings and warnings; and with them He sent the Book in truth to judge between people in matters wherein they differed; but the People of the Book after the clear Signs came to them did not differ among themselves except through selfish contumacy. Allah by His Grace guided the believers to the truth concerning that wherein they differed. For Allah guides whom He will to a path that is straight.[103]

Or (take) the similitude of one who passed by a hamlet all in ruins to its roofs.

He said: "Oh!" "How shall Allah bring it (ever) to life after (this) its death?" But Allah caused him to die for a hundred years then raised him up (again)."

He said: "How long didst thou tarry (thus)?"

He said: "Perhaps a day or part of a day."

He said: "Nay thou hast tarried thus a hundred years; but look at thy food and thy drink; they show no signs of age; and look at thy donkey: and that We may make of thee a Sign unto the people look further at the bones how We bring them together and clothe them with flesh!"

When this was shown clearly to him he said: "I know that Allah hath power over all things."[104]

The parable of those who spend their substance in the way of Allah is that of a grain of corn: it groweth seven ears and each ear hath a hundred grains. Allah giveth manifold increase to whom He pleaseth; and Allah careth for all and He knoweth all things.[105]

Before removing the unbelievers from their dwellings, God warned them, to no avail.

The apostles were sent) thus for thy Lord would not destroy for their wrongdoing men's habitations whilst their occupants were unwarned. To all are degrees (or ranks) according to their deeds: for thy Lord is not unmindful of anything that they do.[106]

Then after him (Noah) We sent (many) apostles to their Peoples: they brought them Clear Signs but they would not believe what they had already rejected beforehand. Thus do We seal the hearts of the transgressors.[107]

The unbelievers would usually prejudge the issues before Prophet Muhammad (pbuh) had a chance to explain them.

Their apostles said: "Is there a doubt about Allah the Creator of the heavens and the earth?" "It is He Who invites you in order that He may forgive you your sins and give you respite for a term appointed!"

They said: "Ah!" "Ye are no more than human like we!" "Ye wish to turn us away from the (gods) our fathers used to worship: then bring us some clear authority."

Their apostles said to them: "True we are human like yourselves but Allah doth grant His grace to such of His servants as He pleases." "It is not for us to bring you an authority except as Allah permits." "And on Allah let all men of faith put their trust." "There is no reason for us not to put our trust on Allah." "Indeed, He has guided us to the Ways we (follow)." "We shall certainly bear with patience all the hurt you may cause us: for those who put their trust should put their trust on Allah."

And the Unbelievers said to their apostles: "Be sure we shall drive you out of our land or ye shall return to our religion."

However, their Lord inspired (this Message) to them: Verily We shall cause the wrongdoers to perish! And verily We shall cause you to abide in the land and succeed them. This for such as fear the time when they shall stand before My tribunal such as fear the punishment denounced. But they sought victory and decision (there and then) and frustration was the Lut of every powerful obstinate transgressor.[108]

(They are) those who if We establish them in the land establish regular prayer and give regular charity enjoin the right and forbid wrong: with Allah rests the end (and decision) of (all) affairs.[109] How many populations have We destroyed which were given to wrong-doing! They tumbled down on their roofs. And how many wells are lying idle and neglected and castles lofty and well-built![110]

And We sent to them an apostle from among themselves saying: "Worship Allah!" "Ye have no other Allah but Him." "Will ye not fear (Him)?"

And the chiefs of his people who disbelieved and denied the Meeting in the Hereafter and on whom We had bestowed the good things of this life said: "He is no more than a man like yourselves; he eats of that of which ye eat and drinks of what ye drink." "If ye obey a man like yourselves behold it is certain ye will be lost." "Does he promise that when ye die and become dust and bones ye shall be brought forth (again)?" "Far very far is that which ye are promised!" "There is nothing but our life in this world!" "We shall die and we live!" "But we shall never be raised up again!" "He is only a man who invents a lie against Allah but we are not the ones to believe in him!"

Muhammad *(pbuh)* said: "O my Lord!" "Help me: for that they accuse me of falsehood."

Allah said: "In but a little while they are sure to be sorry!"

Then the Blast overtook them with justice and We made them as rubbish of dead leaves (floating on the stream of Time)! So away with the people who do wrong! Then We raised after them other generations. No people can hasten their term nor can they delay (it). Then sent We Our apostles in succession: every time there came to a people their apostle they accused him of falsehood: so We made them follow each other (in punishment): We made them as a tale (that is told): so away with a people that will not believe! O ye apostles! Enjoy (all) things good and pure and work righteousness: for I am well acquainted with (all) that ye do. And verily this Brotherhood of yours is a single Brotherhood and I am your Lord and Cherisher: therefore fear Me (and no other).[111]

Before them was denied (the Hereafter) by the people of Noah the Companions of the Rass, the Thamud, the `Ad, Pharaoh, the Brethren of Lut, the Companions of the Wood, and the people of Tubba; each one (of them) rejected the apostles and My warning was duly fulfilled (in them). Were We then weary with the first Creation that they should be in confused doubt about a new

Creation?[112]

One Day everything that can be in commotion will be in violent commotion Followed by oft repeated (commotions): Hearts that Day will be in agitation; Cast down will be (their owners') eyes.

They say (now): "What!" "I shall we indeed be returned to (our) former state?" "What!" "When we shall have become rotten bones?" "... It would in that case be a return with loss!"

However, verily it will be but a single (compelling) Cry. When behold they will be in the (full) awakening (to Judgment).[113]

Say: "Whoever is an enemy to Gabriel for he brings down the (revelation) to thy heart by Allah's will a confirmation of what went before and guidance and glad tidings for those who believe." "Whoever is an enemy to Allah and His angels and apostles to Gabriel and Michael Lo! Allah is an enemy to those who reject faith."[114]

But whosoever turns away from My Message verily for him is a life narrowed down and We shall raise him up blind on the Day of Judgment.

He will say: "O my Lord!" "Why hast thou raised me up blind while I had sight (before)?"

(Allah) will say: "Thus didst thou when Our Signs came unto thee disregard them: so wilt thou this day be disregarded."[115]

Muhammad is not the father of any of your men but (he is) the

Apostle of Allah and the Seal of the Prophets: and Allah has full knowledge of all things.[116]

Finally, Prophet Muhammad *(pbuh)*, God's last and final messenger, was the ultimate icon of peace and mercy to mankind. His words, actions and dealings with all of those around him demonstrate the purity and fine quality of his character. God encourages Muslims to read and to try to understand Prophet Muhammad's *(pbuh)* mission, the Qur'an and His message. This may require several readings and some serious analysis of each verse, coupled with Qur'anic exegesis, as documented by thousands of researchers and scholars. The accumulation of such knowledge will remove any doubt of God being the absolute Creator and re-possessor of man.

In the end, when those in doubt rise above the struggle between the mind and the spirit and learn to devote their lives entirely to God and believe in the Day of Judgment, it may become possible for them to be among those who ultimately join Him in His eternal Dominion. Prophet Muhammad *(pbuh)* was notably in favor of peace and did everything to protect his people and Islam. His message is clear, and his religion, Islam, has been established for those who completely believe in God and his message.

Today, the majority of Muslims yearns for peace during every waking moment of their lives and hope that Prophet Muhammad's *(pbuh)* message will resonate in the minds of the nonbelievers so that they may attain salvation. "The Prophet *(pbuh)* gave man a message of faith, ethics, and hope, in which God reminds all people of His presence, His requirements, and the final Day of Return and Encounter."[117] Countless talks and peace resolutions have and will continue to fail until people learn to love one another as Prophet Muhammad *(pbuh)* has taught his followers to love him and to love God. He taught them to follow his example by turning to God for solutions to all problems and dilemmas. He taught them patience and endurance in the face of calamities and guided them through his wisdom to perfect human relations through peace and negotiation.

Throughout history peace has never been possible without negotiation, and war has never been the goal of any prophet. Prophet Muhammad *(pbuh)* did not build the Ummah or world of Islam overnight, nor did those who came after him. However, today, over a billion Muslims by birth and thousands of converts have submitted their will to Islam in hope for atonement and compensation in the afterlife. The Qur'an itself is a miracle, and its contents are living proof that God is the power above all powers. Believing in God's prophets as the ultimate icons of peace and harmony in this world is the beginning of one's initiation toward the belief in the possibility of eternal peace and deliverance. In the end, believers are the integral figures in voicing Islam as a religion of love and peace. Prophet Muhammad *(pbuh)* lived his life based on Islamic principles, and it is the duty of every Muslim to do the same in order to achieve a life of liberation now and in the hereafter.

Chapter 25

Peace and the Prophets of Islam

This book reveals the stories of Islam's 25 Prophets mentioned in the Qur'an with all verses quoted verbatim. Even though the majority of these stories are mentioned in previous Heavenly Scriptures, God found that some of them were misinterpreted and that it was important to restate them accurately in the Qur'an. This was to reiterate the importance of believing in God, His Oneness and His exigency to create peace among mankind. God communicated with His prophets through visions and angels and not one of them engaged in self-indulgence or supremacy. They were mostly humble and modest. They did their best to advise their people and to accomplish their mission. The prophets of Islam left behind them a religion that promoted love, equality, and peace.

Iblis played a major role in proving that man had the potential to become evil, violent, and hateful. Iblis, who was made of fire, was once, one of God's favorite angels. He worshipped God so intensely that when man was created, he became very jealous. He did not believe that man would worship God the way he did, and he wanted to prove his point to God. He believed that by being created from fire, he was better than anything created from water and clay and that Adam and Eve were inferior to him. Eventually, he led Adam and Eve to eat from the *Forbidden Tree*. As a result, God removed them from the Garden of Eden and placed them on earth. He told them to fend for themselves and deal with the consequences of forgetting about their covenant with Him. Their lives were shattered, and the only way to survive was to endure the hardship of finding food and shelter.

Once Prophet Adam repented and God forgave him, he taught his offspring to believe in God, submit their wills to Him, and to live together peacefully. In fact, Prophet Adam was the first initiator of peace on earth. He explained to his children the importance of living peacefully with one another and the dire consequences of listening to Iblis. Nonetheless, his son Qabil chose to follow the evil path of Iblis and killed his brother Habil out of jealousy. Habil, a firm believer in God, was physically stronger than Qabil and could have struck back, but he chose not to. According to the Qur'an, Qabil was destined to spend his entire life wandering in search for peace and will remain a lost soul even in the afterlife. Qabil's murder of his brother Habil set the path for others to follow and confirmed Iblis's statement to God that man has the potential to commit evil. It is perhaps the temptation and forgetfulness of some men that directs them to forget God and think more of the gratification they receive by satisfying their immediate desires. As a result, the Almighty, most kind and beneficent, decided to continue to give man a chance to be saved and sent hundreds of prophets of which 25 are mentioned in the Qur'an.

Islam's prophets from Adam to Muhammad *(pbuh)* found themselves in confrontational situations with their enemies in the name of God and peace. The main goal of each prophet was to draw people closer to one another and to reinforce the belief in God's Oneness. Iblis continued his work to lead the weak astray and God continued to send His prophets to remind mankind of His existence and the need to worship Him if they wanted to be saved. It was the duty of each prophet to fulfill his individual mission and to spread peace and lead man to the straight path.

From among His prophets, there were those who warned people that trouble was ahead if they did not listen to their advice. For example, Prophet Idris warned his people to believe in God, but they would not listen to him. He was compelled to leave them and go elsewhere. He went to another country and was successful at leading its people to believe in God and to live in peace. Similarly, Prophet Nuh who is said to have lived 950 years, spent many of his years trying to convince his people of the benefits in worshipping God. When Prophet Nuh cried to God in despair, God decided to create a flood and abolish the unbelievers. He instructed Prophet Nuh to build an Ark and to take with him the believers and a male and female animal of every kind. He informed him that once the flood was over, He would deliver them safely ashore. Prophet Nuh's son refused to go with him and was not willing to believe that he could not save himself from God's wrath. To Prophet Nuh's chagrin, God ordered him to leave his son behind since he was a non-believer. Once the Ark landed, God delivered Prophet Nuh and his people to a new, serene world of believers while the unbelievers were drowned.

Prophet Hud also struggled with his people and advised them against idol worship, but they accused him of falsehood even though he explained to them that he was God's sincere and trustworthy advisor. He warned them to worship God so that they may be compensated with abundant rains, but they refused. Their rejection of Prophet Hud and refusal to believe in his message brought the wrath of God upon them. They were overtaken by sterilizing winds while the believers were given the opportunity to find a sense of peace and balance and live in a state of harmony.

When Prophet Salih informed many of his people not to live extravagant lives and to stay away from sin so that God may compensate them with gardens, springs, dates, and palm trees, they refused. An earthquake overtook them, and they remained prostrate in their homes leaving Prophet Salih and the believers to connect and respect one another in peace and harmony.

Prophet Ibrahim and his immediate descendants taught that peace can be achieved through obedience to God. As a child, Prophet Ibrahim found peace in worshipping God and wanted his people to be the same. When they refused and tried to burn him, God protected him by miraculously cooling the fire around him. Nonetheless, they despised him and developed other strategies to kill him. At that point, God inspired him to immigrate to the blessed lands of Syria, Canaan, and Palestine where they lived peacefully with one another and raised new generations of believers. These new generations became the sons and daughters of three living monotheistic religions today, namely, Judaism, Christianity, and Islam. Similarly, Prophet Ibrahim's nephew Prophet Lut, was distressed by those who practiced homosexuality in his town, so God sent two angels to save him from a rain created of brimstones so that he might live peacefully with his family in a new land. Prophet Isma'il, the son of Hajar and Prophet Ibrahim also raised a generation of peaceful believers and agreed to sacrifice his life to God when his father, Prophet Ibrahim informed him of his vision to sacrifice him. When Prophet Ibrahim was ready to comply with God's test of faith, Angel Jibril substituted a lamb instead. Prophet Ibrahim's other son Prophet Ishaq was also a firm believer in God and instructed his family to do the same. He gave birth to Prophet Yaqub who spent his entire life educating his people and his sons to be merciful and kind. Prophet Yaqub had a preference for his son Yusuf since he knew in his heart that God had chosen him to become a prophet. Out of jealousy, the other sons threw Prophet Yusuf into a dry well and led their father to believe that he was eaten by a wolf. Soon thereafter, his cries were heard by travelers who saw him as an opportunity to make money and sold him to the King of Egypt. Prophet Yusuf had many visions and his visions were his door to freedom and success. Eventually, he was able to reunite with his immoral brothers who led him to his aged and grieving father. Peace and happiness were restored, and he lived peacefully with his family and the people of his kingdom. Prophet Ayub, a direct descendant of Prophet Yusuf, worked hard to establish peace among his people and encourage them to believe in God and His kindness. To test Prophet Ayub's patience, God allowed Iblis to inflict him with disease, obliterate his family and lead him into poverty. Once Prophet Ayub passed the test of faith, he was restored. He married, had a new family, and lived a peaceful and harmonious life.

Just as earlier prophets did, Prophet Zul-kifl warned his people that they will never obtain peace if they were not obedient to God. He was a powerful man and a firm believer in God. He spent many years trying to convince idol worshippers to believe in God, but he was unsuccessful. As a result, the unbelievers were overtaken by the Plague leaving the faithful to worship God and live a peaceful and harmonious life. Prophet Musa, the father of Judaism and originator of the Hebraic Scripture was miraculously empowered by God to triumph over the Egyptian Pharaoh and lead the Israelites to safety. He was the only prophet who actually spoke to God without the intervention of angels and visions. With the support of his brother Prophet Harun, their people were given the founding principles of monotheistic faith, and they taught the Israelis the criteria between right and wrong.

Prophet Dawood taught his people how to trust in God and believe in the afterlife and how to deal justly with one another. He taught them to live in peace, set aside their hunger for wealth and prosperity, and devote more time to worshipping God. Similarly, his son, Prophet Suleiman was among the faithful and was empowered by God to communicate with birds and sway the wind to his likening. He converted Bilqis, the Queen of Sheeba to worship God rather than the sun. She found peace from within from the moment she submitted her will to the Almighty. Prophet Dawood also completed the Temple in Jerusalem for the worship of one true God and was considered among the faithful along with his followers.

Prophet Elias was among those who taught peace and reminded his people of God and the importance of worshipping Him. With the exception of a few, they rejected his teachings. As a result, he encouraged the believers to join him in leading a peaceful and pleasant life. They spent the majority of their time praying and submitting their wills to God. Prophet Al-Yasa, his follower, did the same and guided his people to light. God told Prophet Yunus to convince his people to believe in God and subside from idol worshipping, but he lost patience. He was swallowed by a whale and was miraculously saved when he repented and said the words "There is no god, but God." He recovered and guided more than one hundred thousand people to worship God and live in peace. Prophet Zakariah and his son Prophet Yahya were also of God's chosen ones and were able to deter their people from selfishness and insincerity into a life of honesty and peace.

So Zakariah came out to his people from his chamber. He told them by signs to celebrate Allah's praises in the morning and in the evening.[1] So, We listened to him: and We granted him Yahya: We cured his wife's (barrenness) for him. These three were ever

194

quick in emulation in good works: they used to call on Us with love and reverence and humble themselves before Us.[2]

Prophet Issa, whose teachings were used to found Christianity, worked continuously throughout his short life to demonstrate to the Children of Israel that he was an apostle from God and his mission was to confirm the Law which came before him and to make lawful to them some things that were once forbidden. He also gave them glad tidings of an apostle to come after him whose name was Ahmad (or Muhammad *(pbuh)*), but they refused to believe Prophet Issa. His goal was to create a stronger community of believers among the Jews, but to his sorrow, some believed him while others did not.

Finally, according to the Qur'an, Prophet Muhammad *(pbuh)* was the seal of prophets. After him, man will be left to believe or not to believe until the Day of Judgment where God will hold every human being accountable for his righteousness or sins. At the age of forty, Prophet Muhammad *(pbuh)* was a happily married father and successful businessman. After his caravan trips, he frequently camped with his family in the cave of Mount Hira. On the 17th day of Ramadan, 610, Prophet Muhammad *(pbuh)* received his first revelation. He felt the powerful grip of Angel Jibril who demanded that he recite after him. When Prophet Muhammad *(pbuh)* refused, the angel possessed him again with more force and claimed:

Proclaim! (or read!) in the name of thy Lord and Cherisher, Who created- Created man, out of a (mere) clot of congealed blood: Proclaim! And thy Lord is Most Bountiful,- He Who taught (the use of) the pen,- Taught man that which he knew not.[3]

These were the first verses of the Qur'an, but when the Qur'an was gathered into its final Scripture of 114 chapters, these verses were placed at the beginning of chapter 96. It remained in its oral state until some years after the death of Prophet Muhammad *(pbuh)* when it was placed in its final and unchangeable written form. Prophet Muhammad *(pbuh)* memorized God's message and taught it to the believers. Among the first to believe were his wife Khadija, his children and a few family members. He decided to begin the spread of Islam by starting with his own family, the Bani Hashem Clan, who were pagan Arabs. They considered his *self claimed prophecy* to be a joke and did not believe that he was God's chosen one. Eventually, they became his worst enemies. When they realized that Prophet Muhammad's *(pbuh)* followers were growing rapidly, they saw him as a threat to their wealth and control of the city of Mecca. They put a ransom on his life and caused Prophet Muhammad *(pbuh)* and hundreds of his followers to flee Mecca. In fact, Prophet Muhammad *(pbuh)* once found refuge with the Christian King of Abyssinia who welcomed him and was among the first to demonstrate religious tolerance in the name of peace.

Hence, Prophet Muhammad *(pbuh)* set the template for Muslims to conduct their lives and lead the world on the straight path. He fought in self defense and for the survival of God's word. His final sermon to the believers proves this point.

O People
Lend me an attentive ear, for I know not whether after this year, I shall ever be amongst you again. Therefore listen to what I am saying to you very carefully and take these words to those who could not be present here today.

O People
Just as you regard this month, this day, this city as sacred, so regard the life and property of every Muslim as a sacred trust. Return the goods entrusted to you to their rightful owners. Hurt no one so that no one may hurt you. Remember that you will indeed meet your Lord, and that He will indeed reckon your deeds. Allah has forbidden you to take usury (interest); therefore all interest obligation shall henceforth be waived. Your capital, however, is yours to keep. You will neither inflict nor suffer any inequity.

Allah has judged that there shall be no interest and that all interest due to Abbas Ibn 'Abd al Muttalib (the Prophet's uncle) shall henceforth be waived.

Beware of Satan for the safety of your religion. He has lost all hope that he will ever be able to lead you astray in big things, so beware of following him in small things.

O People

It is true that you have certain rights in regard to your women, but they also have rights over you. Remember that you have taken them as your wives, only under Allah's trust and with His permission. If they abide by your right then to them belongs the right to be fed and clothed in kindness. Do treat you women well and be kind to them, for they are your partners and committed helpers. And it is your right that they do not make friends with anyone of whom you do not approve, as well as never to be unchaste.

O People

Listen to me in earnest, worship Allah, say your five daily prayers (Salah), fast during the month of Ramadan, and give your wealth in Zakat.

Perform Hajj if you can afford to.

All mankind is from Adam and Eve, an Arab has no superiority over a non-Arab nor a non-Arab has any superiority over an Arab; also a white has no superiority over a black, nor a black has any superiority over a white- except by piety and good action. Learn that every Muslim is a brother to every Muslim and that the Muslims constitute one brotherhood. Nothing shall be legitimate to a Muslim, which belongs to a fellow Muslim unless it was given freely and willingly. Do not therefore, do injustice to yourselves.

Remember one day you will appear before Allah and answer for your deeds. So beware, do not stray from the path of righteousness after I am gone. People, no prophet or apostle will come after me and no new faith will be born. Reason well therefore, O people, and understand words which I convey to you. I leave behind me two things, the Quran and the Sunnah (Hadith), and if you follow these you will never go astray. All those who listen to me shall pass on my words to others and those to others again; and may the last ones understand my words better than those who listened to me directly. Be my witness, O Allah, that I have conveyed your message to your people.[4]

Islam is recognized as a religion free of racism and intolerance, and today, the majority of the 1.3 billion Muslims who believe in the Qur'an's scriptures and obey its laws have adopted the urgency to pursue peace between themselves and the rest of the world. The words "Bismillah Al-Rahman Al-Rahim" or "In the name of God, Most Gracious, Most Merciful" introduce each chapter in the Qur'an only to confirm that God is beneficent and forgiving. Also, religion is not necessarily the founder of wars as some might believe. God's prophets have proven that war is not the primary solution to misunderstandings and disagreements between tribes and nations. Any war that took place between Muslims and non-Muslims were defensive wars, and terrorists who battle in the name of Islam seem not to understand the true intent of Islam. With the exception of the ignorant, Muslims do not want to convert non-Muslims to Islam, nor do they uphold that their religion is supreme to others. Those who join Islam, do so willingly since according to the Qur'an there is "no compulsion in religion" and as long as people submit their wills to God, God alone, will evaluate their actions on the Day of Judgment.

> "Those who believe (in the Qur'an), and those who follow the Jewish (scriptures), and the Christians and the Sabians,- any who believe in Allah and the Last Day, and work righteousness, shall have their reward with their Lord; on them shall be no fear, nor shall they grieve."[5]

There is no doubt that He will extend His mercy on the faithful regardless of their religion, race, or gender and a thorough and comprehensive reading of the Qur'an will demonstrate that God does not judge monotheistic believers based on their religion, race, or gender.

Men and women were created to compliment one another and to

educate their progeny to observe the laws of the Heavenly Scriptures and to respect their friends and neighbors, and to refrain from evil doings. Those who commit evil deeds and act out of self-interest and voracity will find themselves wrapped in eternal wars of hatred and transgression. Since the three monotheistic religions believe in the same God and possess scriptures that compliment one another, then, ministries should set aside religious differences and find ways to discuss and negotiate terms to create peace worldwide. Muslims believe that the Hebraic Bible, the Old Testament, the New Testament, and the Qur'an are collections of written revelations and that the Qur'an is God's final message to mankind. Many monotheistic preachers have begun the peace process by creating inter-religious peace talks to eradicate spiritual misconceptions and encourage religious tolerance. Open dialogues, comparative religious studies, and interfaith discussions are encouraged and promoted by numerous religious leaders around the world. Their goal is to preach tolerance and understanding, and acceptance of other faiths.

Many peace organizations around the world are interested in Islamic peace issues since relations between the East and the West have become polarized. In order to overcome this polarization, it is crucial to encourage moderation rather than extremism and to contribute to the promotion of peace and interest in the understanding of monotheistic religions rather than search for theological justification to kill and control those who shake the spiritual status quo of the other. Islam is a powerful and peaceful religion and by reading the stories of the prophets one may learn more about Islam and develop a greater degree of religious tolerance and desire for global alliance.

GLOSSARY

Arabic—English

(pbuh)	Peace be upon him (used when Prophet Muhammad's name is mentioned)
Ad People	People who lived in Southern Arabia
Adam	Man (meaning in Arabic)
Ahl Al-Kitab	People of the Book (Christians, Jews, and Muslims)
Al-Alaq	The 96th sura or chapter of the Qur'an
Al-Kitab	God's Heavenly Scriptures
Ar-rih al-aqim	Sterilizing wind
Bakka	Ancient name of Mecca, Saudi Arabia
Baal	An ancient idol
Bismillah Al-Rahman Al-Rahim	In the name of God, Most Gracious, Most Merciful Dirham Money
Eid ul-Adha	Holiday celebrated by all Muslims on the last of pilgrimage.
Habil	Abel (Adam's son—Bible)
Hadith	Commentaries

Hajj	The Hajj is the pilgrimage to Mecca taken at a specific time during the year. It is the fifth pillar of Islam and is required of all able-bodied Muslims to carry out at least once in a lifetime if they can afford to do so.
Haneef	One who is upright
Hannah	Anne—Bible
Hawaa	Eve—Bible
Hijra	The emigration of Prophet Muhammad *(pbuh)* and his followers to the city of Medina in 622 CE. This marked the first year of the Islamic calendar.
Hira	Cave in Mecca where Prophet Muhammad received his first revelation.
Hudaybiyya	The treaty that took place between the state of Medina and the Quraish of Mecca in 628 CE.
Iblis	Satan—Bible
Ifrit	A Jinn or spirit
Iqra	To read or proclaim
Jahiliya	Age of ignorance
Jibril	Archangel Gabriel—Bible
Jihad	Holy struggle or to strive
Jinn	One of a class of spirits that according to Muslim demonology inhabit the earth, assume various forms, and exercise supernatural power
Kabaa (Al Masjid Al-Haram) Saudi Arabia.	The Kabaa is a cube shaped building in Mecca, It was built by Prophet Ibrahim And his son Isma'il and considered to be to most sacred site in Islam. It is at this site that Muslims perform the pilgrimage.

Khandaq	Trench
Khaybar	Fortified City, Saudi Arabia
Kifl	Double or duplicate
La illaha ila Allah wa Muhammad *(pbuh)* Rasoul Allah	There is no god, but God and Muhammad is His messenger
Lawh Mahfouz	Protected Tablet of God—The Qur'an
Mariam	Mary—Bible
Marwah	Hill in Mecca, Saudi Arabia
Masjid al-Taqwa	The Mosque of Piety
Moriah	The hill near which stands the Dome of the Rock in Jerusalem
Mu'ammar	The long lived
Muslim	One who submits his/her will to God, believes in His Oneness and in Muhammad as His final prophet
Qabil	Cain (Adam's son—Bible)
Qarya	Village
Quraish	Prophet Muhammad's *(pbuh)* kinsmen
Rajab	A month in the Islamic calendar
Rasoul Allah	God's messenger (Muhammad) *(pbuh)*
Safa	Hill in Mecca, Saudi Arabia
Sunnah Al Rasoul	By example of the Prophet Muhammad *(pbuh)*
Sura	Chapter—Qur'an
Thamud people	Ancient people of Hejar, a town between Syria and Hejaz
Tuwa	Sacred valley near Mt. Sinai in the Middle East.
Ummah	Followers of Islam
Umrah	It is a pilgrimage to Mecca that Muslims can take at any time during the year. It is recommended, but not compulsory in Islam.

Yathrib	The current city of Medina in Saudi Arabia
Zama	Draw together
Zamzam	Holy water spring in Mecca

GLOSSARY

English—Arabic

A month in the Islamic calendar	Rajab
A spirit	Ifrit
Abel—Bible	Habil (Adam's son)
Age of Ignorance	Jahiliya
God's Heavenly Scriptures	Al-Kitab
An ancient idol	Baal
An ancient people in Saudi Arabia	Ad People
An ancient people of Hejar, a town between Syria and Hejaz	Thamud people
Ancient name of Mecca, Saudi Arabia	Bakka
Anne—Bible	Hannah
By example of the Prophet Muhammad *(pbuh)*	Sunnah Al Rasoul
Cain	Qabil (Adam's son)
Cave in Mecca where Prophet Muhammad *(pbuh)* received his revelation	Hira

Chapter—Qur'an	Sura
Commentaries	Hadith
Double or duplicate	Kifl
Draw together	Zama
Emigration	Hijra
Eve	Hawaa
Followers of Islam	Ummah
Fortified city of Saudi Arabia	Khaybar
Archangel Gabriel	Jibril
God's messenger (Muhammad)	Rasoul Allah
The Hajj is the pilgrimage to Mecca. It is the fifth pillar of Islam and is required of all able-bodied Muslims to carry out at least once in a lifetime if they can afford to do so.	Hajj
It is a pilgrimage to Mecca that Muslims can take at any time during the year. It is recommended, but not compulsory in Islam. Hill in Mecca, Saudi Arabia	Umrah
Hill in Mecca, Saudi Arabia	Safa
Hill in Mecca, Saudi Arabia	Marwah
Holiday celebrated by all Muslims on the last of pilgrimage	Eid ul-Adha
Holy struggle or to strive	Jihad
Holy water spring in Mecca	Zamzam
In the name of God, Most Gracious, Most Merciful	Bismillah Al-Rahman Al-Rahim
Man	Adam
Mary—Bible	Mariam
Money	Dirham
Muhammad *(pbuh)* kinsmen	Quraish

One of a class of spirits that according to Muslim demonology inhabit the earth, assume various forms, and exercise supernatural power	*Jinn*
One who is upright	Haneef
One who submits his/her will to God and believes in His Oneness	Muslim
Peace be upon he (used when Prophet Muhammad's name is mentioned)	*(pbuh)*
People of the Book (Christians, Jews, and Muslims)	Ahl Al-Kitab
Protected Tablet of God—The Qur'an	Lawh Mahfouz
Sacred valley near Mt. Sinai in the Middle East	Tuwa
Satan	Iblis
Sterilizing wind	Ar-rih al-aqim
The current city of Medina in Saudi Arabia	Yathrib
The emigration of Prophet Muhammad *(pbuh)* and his followers to the city of Medina in 622 CE. This marked the first year of the Islamic calendar	Hijra
The hill near which stands the Dome of the Rock in Jerusalem	Moriah
The Kabaa is a cube shaped building in Mecca, Saudi Arabia. It was built by Prophet Ibrahim and his son Isma'il and considered to be to most sacred site in Islam. It is at this site that Muslims perform the pilgrimage.	Kabaa (Al Masjid Al-Haram)
The long-lived	Mu'ammar
The 96th sura or chapter of the Qur'an	Al-Alaq

The Mosque of Piety (Saudi Arabia)	Masjid al-Taqwa
The treaty that took place between the state of Medina and the Quraish of Mecca in 628 CE.	Hudaybiyya
There is no god, but God and Muhammad is His messenger	La illaha ila Allah wa Muhammad Rasoul Allah
To read or proclaim	Iqra
Trench	Khandaq
Village	Qarya

Prophets in the Qur'an	Prophet names mentioned in the Bible
Prophet Adam	Adam
Prophet Idris	Enoch
Prophet Nuh	Noah
Prophet Hud	Qur'an only
Prophet Salih	Qur'an only
Prophet Ibrahim	Abraham
Prophet Lut	Lot
Prophet Isma'il	Ishmael
Prophet Ishaq	Issac
Prophet Yaqub	Jacob
Prophet Yusuf	Joesph
Prophet Shuaib	Qur'an only
Prophet Ayub	Job
Prophet Zul-kifl	Ezekiel
Prophet Musa	Moses
Prophet Harun	Aaron
Prophet Dawood	David
Prophet Suleiman	Solomon
Prophet Elias	Elijah
Prophet Al-Yasa	Elisha
Prophet Yunus	Jonah
Prophet Zakariah	Zachary
Prophet Yahya	John the Baptist
Prophet Issa	Jesus
Muhammad *(pbuh)*	Ahmad *(pbuh)*

Notes

Table of Contents

Acknowledgments

1   Ali, Yusuf A. The Holy Qur'an: Text, Translation, and Commentary. United States: McGregor & Werner, Inc. 1946. 13:23-24.

Introduction

1   Qur'an 3:81.
2   Qur'an 29:46.
3   Stowasser, Barbara F. *Women in the Qur'an, Traditions, Translations, and Interpretations.* New York: Oxford University Press, 1994. pp. 13–14.
4   Ibid., pp. 15–18.

Chapter 1: Prophet Adam—Adam

1   Qur'an 2:35.
2   Qur'an 20:120–121.
3   Qur'an 41:9.
4   Qur'an 50:38.
5   Qur'an 57:4.
6   Qur'an 25:59.
7   Qur'an 41:10–12.
8   Qur'an 17:44.
9   Ali, Yusuf A. *The Holy Qur'an: Text, Translation, and Commentary.* 1946. pp. 484–485.

10   Qur'an 2:30.
11   Qur'an 15:28.
12   Qur'an 15:27.
13   Qur'an 38:72.
14   Qur'an 2:30.
15   Qur'an 2:34.
16   Qur'an 15:31.
17   Qur'an 18:50.
18   Qur'an 15:32.
19   Qur'an 38:75.
20   Qur'an 7:12.
21   Qur'an 15:33.
22   Qur'an 38:77–81.
23   Qur'an 17:63-65.
24   Qur'an 15:39–40.
25   Qur'an 7:16–17.
26   Qur'an 15:41–44.
27   Qur'an 7:18.
28   Qur'an 2:31–33.
29   Qur'an 2:35.
30   Ali, Yusuf A. *The Holy Qur'an: Text, Translation, and Commentary.* pp. 24–30.
31   Qur'an 7:20–21.
32   Qur'an 2:36.
33   Qur'an 20:115–121.
34   Qur'an 7:22–25.
35   Qur'an 2:37–39.
36   Qur'an 7:26–27.
37   Qur'an 7:35.
38   Qur'an 7:54.
39   Qur'an 5:27-31.
40   Qur'an 5:32.
41   Qur'an 4:1.
42   Qur'an 10:3.
43   Qur'an 10:5.
44   Qur'an 11:7.
45   Qur'an 16:3–4.
46   Qur'an 35:11.
47   Qur'an 39:6.
48   Qur'an 40:67.
49   Qur'an 25:54.
50   Qur'an 76:2.
51   Qur'an 86:5–7.
52   Qur'an 30:54.
53   Qur'an 22:5.

54 Qur'an 53:45–46.
55 Qur'an 16:5–21.
56 Qur'an 16:66–81.
57 Qur'an 9:36.
58 Qur'an 17:66.
59 Qur'an 17:70.
60 Qur'an 22:6.
61 Qur'an 22:17.
62 Qur'an 25:33.
63 Qur'an 46:15.
64 Qur'an 49:13.
65 Qur'an 55:1–8.
66 Qur'an 55:14–15.
67 Qur'an 53:43–44.
68 Qur'an 55:17.
69 Qur'an 55:19–20.
70 Qur'an 56:57–59.
71 Ali, Yusuf A. *The Holy Qur'an: Text, Translation, and Commentary.* p. 1474.
72 Qur'an 75:36–40.

Chapter2: Prophet Idris—Enoch

1 Qur'an 21:85.
2 Qur'an 19:56-57.
3 Al Jibouri, Yasin T. *The Concept of God in Islam.* Islamic Republic Of Iran: Ansariyan Publications, 2002. *p. 241–248.*
4 Ibid. pp. 246–247.

Chapter 3: Prophet Nuh—Noah

1 Ali, Yusuf A. *The Holy Qur'an: Text, Translation, and Commentary.* pp. 522–527.
2 Ibid. pp. 248-251.
3 Ibid. p. 257.
4 Qur'an 29:14.
5 Qur'an 23:23–25.
6 Qur'an 11:25–35.
7 Qur'an 10:71–72.
8 Qur'an 7:59–63.
9 Qur'an 26:105–118.
10 Qur'an 71:1–28.
11 Qur'an 11:36.
12 Qur'an 23:38.
13 Qur'an 23:27–29.
14 Qur'an 11:38–41.

15 Qur'an 11:45-47.
16 Qur'an 54:10–14.
17 Qur'an 11:42–44.
18 Qur'an 54:15.
19 Qur'an 37:75.
20 Qur'an 71:25.
21 Qur'an 37:76–81.
22 Qur'an 7:64.
23 Qur'an 10:73.
24 Qur'an 11:48.
25 Qur'an 17:3.
26 Qur'an 17:17.
27 Qur'an 11:49.
28 Qur'an 25:37.
29 Qur'an 66:10.
30 Qur'an 40:5–6.
31 Qur'an 23:30–35.
32 Qur'an 23:40–41.

Chapter 4: Prophet Hud

1   Ali, Yusuf A. *The Holy Qur'an: Text, Translation, and Commentary.* p. 358.
2   Qur'an 29:38.
3   Qur'an 11:50.
4   Qur'an 26:124–135.
5   Qur'an 26:136–138.
6   Qur'an 11:51–52.
7   Qur'an 7:67–71.
8   Qur'an 11:53–57.
9   Qur'an 46:22–23.
10 Qur'an 41:15–16.
11 Qur'an 46:24–25.
12 Qur'an 54:20.
13 Qur'an 51:42.
14 Qur'an 7:72.

Chapter 5: Prophet Salih

1   Ali, Yusuf A. *The Holy Qur'an: Text, Translation, and Commentary.* pp. 964–972.
2   Qur'an 11:61.
3   Qur'an 26:142–154.
4   Qur'an 27:45–50.
5   Qur'an 11:61–64.
6   Qur'an 54:28.

7   Qur'an 11:65.
8   Qur'an 7:79.
9   Qur'an 11:66–68.
10   Qur'an 15:81–84.
11   Qur'an 17:59–60.

Chapter 6: Prophet Ibrahim—Abraham

1   Ali, Yusuf A. *The Holy Qur'an: Text, Translation, and Commentary.* pp. 51-53.
2   Qur'an 19:41.
3   Qur'an 2:124.
4   Qur'an 21:51.
5   Qur'an 2:131.
6   Qur'an 6:75–79.
7   Qur'an 6:74.
8   Qur'an 6:80–81.
9   Qur'an 26:71–89.
10   Qur'an 19:42–48.
11   Qur'an 21:52–67.
12   Qur'an 37:86–90.
13   Qur'an 9:114.
14   Qur'an 37:91–96.
15   Qur'an 43:26–29.
16   Qur'an 37:97.
17   Qur'an 29:24–-25.
18   Qur'an 21:68.
19   Qur'an 29:24.
20   Qur'an 21:69–73.
21   Qur'an 29:16–18.
22   Qur'an 29:26–27.
23   Qur'an 19:50.
24   Qur'an 2:258.
25   Qur'an 2:260.
26   Qur'an 60:4–6.
27   Qur'an 37:100 -101.
28   Qur'an 11:69.
29   Qur'an 15:53.
30   Qur'an 11:71–73.
31   Qur'an 15:56–57.
32   Qur'an 11:70.
33   Qur'an 51:32–34.
34   Qur'an 11:74–76.
35   Qur'an 51:35–37.
36   Qur'an 14:35–37.

37   Qur'an 14:38–41.
38   Qur'an 37:102–113.
39   Qur'an 3:65–68.
40   Qur'an 3:95.
41   Qur'an 6:82–84.
42   Qur'an 16:120–124.
43   Qur'an 3:96–97.
44   Qur'an 2:125–130.
45   Qur'an 22:26.
46   Qur'an 22:78.
47   Qur'an 38:45–48.
48   Qur'an 2:132–133.

Chapter 7: Prophet Lut—Lot

1   Ali, Yusuf A. *The Holy Qur'an: Text, Translation, and Commentary*. pp.
       646–650.
2   Qur'an 29:31–32.
3   Qur'an 21:160–163.
4   Qur'an 29:29.
5   Qur'an 26:164–169.
6   Qur'an 11:77.
7   Qur'an 15:62–64.
8   Qur'an 15:68–70.
9   Qur'an 11:78–80.
10   Qur'an 15:59-60.
11   Qur'an 11:81–83.
12   Qur'an 15:75–77.
13   Qur'an 27:55–56.

Chapter 8: Prophet Isma'il—Ishmael

1   Qur'an 37:100–101.
2   Qur'an 14:37.
3   Al-Tabatabi, Mohamed H. *Tarikh Al-Inbiyaa*. Beirut: Alaalami Library,
       2002. pp. 151–168.
4   Qur'an 37:102–113.
5   Qur'an 2:127–128.
6   Qur'an 3:65–68.

Chapter 9: Prophet Ishaq—Issac

1   Qur'an 15:53-54.
2   Qur'an 11:71–73.
3   Qur'an 15:55

4   El-Zein, Samih A. *Isaac, Yacob, Yousef, Ayoub, Shuaib*. Beirut: Dar Al-Kitab Allubnani, 1983.

5   Ali, Yusuf A. *The Holy Qur'an: Text, Translation, and Commentary*. pp. 1202–1207.

Chapter 10: Prophet Yaqub—Jacob

1   Qur'an 2:130-140.

2   Qur'an 16:119–123.

Chapter 11: Prophet Yusuf—Joseph

1   Ali, Yusuf A. *The Holy Qur'an: Text, Translation, and Commentary*. pp. 548–549.

2   Ibid. pp. 588–589.

3   Qur'an 12:4-104.

Chapter 12: Prophet Shuaib

1   Ali, Yusuf A. *The Holy Qur'an: Text, Translation, and Commentary*. p. 365.

2   Qur'an 7:85–89.

3   Qur'an 11:86–93.

4   Qur'an 26:177–191.

5   Qur'an 7:90–95.

6   Qur'an 11:94–95.

Chapter 13: Prophet Ayub—Job

1   Ali, Yusuf A. *The Holy Qur'an: Text, Translation, and Commentary*. p. 840.

2   Qur'an 38:41.

3   Qur'an 21:83.

4   Qur'an 38:42–44.

5   Qur'an 21:84.

6   Qur'an 6:83–84.

7   Qur'an 21:81–83.

Chapter 14: Prophet Zul-kifl—Ezekiel

1   Qur'an 21:85–86.

2   Qur'an 38:45-48.

Chapter 15: Prophets Musa & Harun—Moses & Aaron

1   Ali, Yusuf A. *The Holy Qur'an: Text, Translation, and Commentary*. pp. 51–61; 103–137; 792–811.

2   Qur'an 19:51.
3   Qur'an 28:2.
4   Qur'an 6:154.
5   Qur'an 2:62.
6   Qur'an 28:4–21.
7   Qur'an 18:60-82.
8   Qur'an 28:23–30.
9   Qur'an 20:12–16.
10 Qur'an 20:40.
11 Qur'an 20:41.
12 Qur'an 20:17–20.
13 Qur'an 27:10.
14 Qur'an 28:31–35.
15 Qur'an 20:42–48.
16 Qur'an 28:36–39.
17 Qur'an 20:49–59.
18 Qur'an 26:17–45.
19 Qur'an 20:70–73.
20 Qur'an 7:127–135.
21 Qur'an 29:39–40.
22 Qur'an 28:76–81.
23 Qur'an26:52–69.
24 Qur'an 7:160–171.
25 Qur'an 7:138–147.
26 Qur'an 14:5–8.
27 Qur'an 2:50–53.
28 Qur'an 20:83–98.
29 Qur'an 2:54.
30 Qur'an 2:55–61.
31 Qur'an 2:63–74.
32 Qur'an 5:22–25.
33 Qur'an 21:48.
34 Qur'an 20:80–82.
35 Qur'an 2:108.
36 Qur'an 11:96-98.
37 Qur'an 66:11.
38 Qur'an 4:164.
39 Qur'an 5:47.
40 Qur'an 69:9–10.

Chapter 16 Prophet Dawood—David

1   Qur'an 2:246.
2   Ali, Yusuf A. *The Holy Qur'an: Text, Translation, and Commentary.* pp. 98–99.

3 Qur'an 2:246–251.
4 Ali, Yusuf A. *The Holy Qur'an: Text, Translation, and Commentary.* p. 839.
5 Qur'an 6:83-84.
6 Qur'an 21:78.
7 Ali, Yusuf A. *The Holy Qur'an: Text, Translation, and Commentary.* p. 840.
8 Qur'an 38:17–20.
9 Qur'an 2:249–252.
10 Qur'an 38:21–26.
11 Qur'an 38:39–40.

Chapter 17: Prophet Suleiman—Solomon

1 Ali, Yusuf A. *The Holy Qur'an: Text, Translation, and Commentary.* pp. 980-984.
2 Qur'an 38:30–38.
3 Qur'an 2:101–103.
4 Qur'an 21:79–82.
5 Qur'an 27:15–44.
6 Ali, Yusuf A. *The Holy Qur'an: Text, Translation, and Commentary.* pp. 985–989.
7 Qur'an 34:12–21.

Chapter 18: Prophet Elias—Elijah

1 Ali, Yusuf A. *The Holy Qur'an: Text, Translation, and Commentary.* pp. 1203-1209.
2 Qur'an 37:123–132.

Chapter 19: Prophet Al-Yasa—Elisha

1 Qur'an 38:48.
2 Qur'an 6:85–87.
3 Ali, Yusuf A. *The Holy Qur'an: Text, Translation, and Commentary.* p. 312.

Chapter 20: Prophet Yunus—Jonah

1 Ali, Yusuf A. *The Holy Qur'an: Text, Translation, and Commentary.* p. 842.
2 Qur'an 21:87.
3 Qur'an 37:139–148.
4 Qur'an 10:98–99.

Chapter 21: Prophet Zakariah—Zachary

1   Ali, Yusuf A. *The Holy Qur'an: Text, Translation, and Commentary.* p. 133.
2   Qur'an 19:2–11.
3   Qur'an 21:90.
4   Qur'an 3:37.

Chapter 22: Prophet Yahya—John the Baptist

1   Ali, Yusuf A. *The Holy Qur'an: Text, Translation, and Commentary.* p. 769-770.
2   Qur'an 19:7.
3   Qur'an 19:12–15.

Chapter 23: Prophet Issa—Jesus

1   Ali, Yusuf A. *The Holy Qur'an: Text, Translation, and Commentary.* p. 230.
2   Qur'an 3:35-36.
3   Ali, Yusuf A. *The Holy Qur'an: Text, Translation, and Commentary.* p. 132.
4   Qur'an 3:36.
5   Qur'an 3:42–51.
6   Qur'an 43:57-60.
7   Ali, Yusuf A. *The Holy Qur'an: Text, Translation, and Commentary.* p. 1336.
8   Qur'an 43:61.
9   Ali, Yusuf A. *The Holy Qur'an: Text, Translation, and Commentary.* p. 1337.
10   Qur'an 43:62–66.
11   Qur'an 61:6.
12   Qur'an 3:52–55.
13   Qur'an 3:59.
14   Ali, Yusuf A. *The Holy Qur'an: Text, Translation, and Commentary.* p. 138.
15   Ibid. p. 230.
16   Qur'an 4:157–159.
17   Qur'an 4:171–172.
18   Ali, Yusuf A. *The Holy Qur'an: Text, Translation, and Commentary.* p. 234.
19   Qur'an 5:78.
20   Qur'an 5:112–120.
21   Qur'an 61:14.
22   Qur'an 66:12.
23   Qur'an 23:50.

24 Qur'an 2:87.
25 Qur'an 2:116.
26 2:253.

Chapter 24: Prophet Muhammad (pbuh)

1 Qur'an 33:40.
2 Al Jibouri, Yasin T. *The Concept of God in Islam.* Islamic Republic Of Iran: Ansariyan Publications, 2002. *pp. 494–523.*
3 Qur'an 61:6.
4 Aslan, Reza. *No god but God.* New York: Random House Inc., 2005. *pp. 33–35.*
5 Qur'an 45:24.
6 Qur'an 96:1–19.
7 Aslan, Reza *(2005). No god but God. Random House Inc. New York. pp* 24–32.
8 Al Jibouri, Yasin T. *The Concept of God in Islam.* Islamic Republic Of Iran: Ansariyan Publications, 2002. *pp. 563–569.*
9 Ibid. pp. 584–591.
10 Qur'an 9:40.
11 Aslan, Reza *(2005). No god but God. Random House Inc. New York. pp. 56–57.*
12 Qur'an 4:3.
13 Qur'an 4:129.
14 Al Jibouri, Yasin T. *The Concept of God in Islam.* Islamic Republic Of Iran: Ansariyan Publications, 2002. *pp. 626–632.*
15 Qur'an 17:81.
16 Aslan, Reza. *No god but God.* New York: Random House Inc., 2005. *pp. 107–110.*
17 Qur'an 2:209.
18 Qur'an 2:111.
19 Qur'an 2:136.
20 Qur'an 2:285.
21 Qur'an 3:3.
22 Qur'an 3:7.
23 Qur'an 3:70.
24 Qur'an 3:71.
25 Qur'an 73:15.
26 Qur'an 21:5.
27 Qur'an 3:79.
28 Qur'an 3:144.
29 Qur'an 3:161.
30 Qur'an 3:164.
31 Qur'an 6:48.
32 Qur'an 10:2.

33   Qur'an 10:37.

34   Qur'an 10:41.

35   Qur'an 2:29.

36   Qur'an 17:1.

37   Qur'an 53:2–17.

38   Qur'an 17:9.

39   Qur'an 17:45–46.

40   Qur'an 39:27.

41   Qur'an 40:14–15.

42   Qur'an 40:51–52.

43   Qur'an 48:29.

44   Qur'an 4:69.

45   Qur'an 4:166.

46   Qur'an 3:61.

47   Qur'an 3:64.

48   Qur'an 3:73.

49   Qur'an 3:81.

50   Qur'an 3:84.

51   Qur'an 3:183.

52   Qur'an 6:14–15.

53   Qur'an 6:19.

54   Qur'an 6:50.

55   Qur'an 6:161.

56   Qur'an 7:158.

57   Qur'an 7:187–188.

58   Qur'an 10:38.

59   Qur'an 17:88.

60   Qur'an 10:49.

61   Qur'an 10:104.

62   Qur'an 10:108.

63   Qur'an 17:95–96.

64   Qur'an 17:107-108.

65   Qur'an 18:109–110.

66   Qur'an 46:9–10.

67   Qur'an 38:86–88.

68   Qur'an 52:31.

69   Qur'an 3:72.

70   Qur'an 3:68-69.

71   Qur'an 3:78.

72   Qur'an 3:184.

73   Qur'an 4:105.

74   Qur'an 4:113.

75   Qur'an 6:7–10.

76   Qur'an 6:156–158.

77   Qur'an 7:2.

78 Qur'an 10:61.

79 Qur'an 10:94.

80 Qur'an 10:109.

81 Qur'an 11:12–14.

82 Qur'an 11:17.

83 Qur'an 12:3–4.

84 Qur'an 14:4.

85 Qur'an 16:64.

86 Qur'an 16:103.

87 Qur'an 17:82.

88 Qur'an 17:90–92.

89 Qur'an 17:94.

90 Qur'an 17:105–106.

91 Qur'an 18:54.

92 Qur'an 19:97.

93 Qur'an 20:2–3.

94 Qur'an 20:113.

95 Qur'an 39:28.

96 Qur'an 46:11.

97 Qur'an 52:29–30.

98 Qur'an 52:32–41.

99 Ali, Yusuf A. *The Holy Qur'an: Text, Translation, and Commentary.* p. 503.

100 Qur'an 10:74.

101 Qur'an 6:85–90.

102 Qur'an 3:81–84.

103 Qur'an 2:213.

104 Qur'an 2:259.

105 Qur'an 2:261.

106 Qur'an 6:131–132.

107 Qur'an 10:74.

108 Qur'an 14:10–15.

109 Qur'an 22:41.

110 Qur'an 22:45.

111 Qur'an 23:32–52.

112 Qur'an 50:12–15.

113 Qur'an 79:6–14.

114 Qur'an 2:97–98.

115 Qur'an 20:124–126.

116 Qur'an 33:40.

117 Ramadan, Tareq. *In the Footsteps of the Prophet – Lessons from the Life of Muhammad.* New York: Oxford University Press, 2007. p. 214.

Chapter 25: Peace and the Prophets of Islam

1 Qur'an 19:2–11.
2 Qur'an 21:90.
3 Qur'an 96:1-5.
4 Rogerson, Barnaby. 2003. *The Prophet Muhammad, A Biography.* Great Britain: Little Brown.pp. 207-209
5 Qur'an 2:62.